The Bisbee Stairs:
Exploring the Stairways, Trails, and Hidden Corners of Bisbee, Arizona

Also by David Ryan

The Gentle Art of Wandering

*Long Distance Hiking
on the Appalachian Trail
for the Older Adventurer*

The Bisbee Stairs:
Exploring the Stairways, Trails, and Hidden Corners of Bisbee, Arizona

By David Ryan

New Mountain Books,
Albuquerque, New Mexico

The Bisbee Stairs:
Exploring the Stairways, Trails, and Hidden Corners of Bisbee, Arizona

Copyright © 2014 by David Ryan

ALL RIGHTS RESERVED

No part of this book may be reproduced or transmitted in any form, or by any electronic, mechanical, or other means including photocopying, recording, or by information storage or retrieval system, which includes unauthorized posting on the world wide web or internet in any form, without permission in writing from the publisher, except for brief quotations embodied in literary articles or reviews.

First Edition 2014

10 9 8 7 6 5 4 3 2 1

Library of Congress Catalog Card Number: 2014913162

ISBN: 978-09776968-3-3

New Mountain Books and the author assume no liability for accidents happening to, or injuries sustained by, readers who engage in the activities described in this book.

All GPS coordinates referenced in the book use WGS 84 datum

Photographs: David Ryan, except where noted

Book Design/Production: Carolyn Ryan

Typeface: Garamond, Gill Sans

Published By:

New Mountain Books
2324 Rio Grande Boulevard NW
Albuquerque, New Mexico 87104 USA
612-889-9640
www.newmountainbooks.com

Table of Contents

Section 1 – Bisbee and Its Stairways	3
Section 2 – Touring the Bisbee Stairways	21
Section 3 – Hikes from the Bisbee Trailheads	85
Afterword or How This Book Came to Be	93
Acknowledgements	97

The Bisbee Stairs:
Exploring the Stairways, Trails, and Hidden Corners of Bisbee, Arizona

Bisbee and Its Pit

Section 1

Bisbee and Its Stairways

Bisbee, tucked in the Mule Mountains of southeast Arizona, is more than an old mining town and tourist destination. It is an incredible place to explore on foot. The hilly setting is amazing with gorgeous views no matter which way you turn. The original part of town is so compact that you can walk from one end to the other in less than an hour. And even better there is something special no matter which way you turn. It may be the most interesting small town in America.

By all means take a look at the huge open-pit mine; visit the old underground mine and the historical museum; browse through the stores and galleries on Main Street; take a historical tour; get a bite to eat at one of the town's many restaurants; and stay at one of the local lodges. But once you stop to take a breath, consider stepping away from the crowds and start walking.

What you'll find is the funkiest town in all of America. You'll find folk art and personalized yards and decorated houses everywhere you turn. You'll feel like you're walking through a three-dimensional outdoor art exhibit of personalized yards and houses. You might even feel like you are passing from one personal Shangri-La to another. If you're not clear about the definition of funky, you'll know it when you finish your walk.

If you like to climb public stairways, you're home. You can't get anywhere in "old" Bisbee without stepping on a stair. There are stairs to get you from the street to the sidewalk. Even some of the sidewalks are stairs. You'll find that the only way to get from a street to most houses is to climb some stairs. You'll also discover stairways to get you to the next street. And you'll even see that many of the stairways are the street with five, six, or more levels of houses on the stairway. Some of the stairways lead to sidewalks or trails that go on to more houses.

These stairways are not only short cuts; they are in many places the only way to get around and are the transportation network for this very hilly town. There are so many stairs in old Bisbee that the U. S. Postal Service considers mail to be undeliverable. Everyone is given a post office box and has to go the post office to pick up their mail. Even the old four-story high school gets into the act by having a ground level entrance at every floor.

This book was written to help you find these stairways and the many hidden Shangri-Las of Bisbee. You'll even learn where to find hiking trails to take you high into the hills above Bisbee.

As you use this guide, please remember that you are walking through a real living and breathing community. Bisbee is not a museum or a theme park. If you keep this mind, you'll be rewarded with an amazing adventure and may even be tempted to move to Bisbee and live here yourself.

Bisbee

Before exploring the hidden corners of Bisbee, it makes sense to know a little bit about its setting and story and how the stairs came to be. The Bisbee you see today is dominated by an enormous inactive open-pit copper mine that is almost a mile long, a half mile across, and over 900 feet deep. There is no way you can miss it. The brilliant colors of the layers of rock surrounding the pit alone are worth the trip.

Those houses are not nestled next to a hill; that's an ore dump behind them!

No matter how many times you take a picture of the

pit, the picture won't do it justice. The brilliance of the coppery red layer, the blue gray layer, and the various shades of yellow, gold, and purple just don't come out the same in a picture. You're better off just letting your eyes take it all in as the sunlight plays on the different layers of rock.

The City of Bisbee is located on both sides of the pit. Because of the pit and other mining infrastructure the city is cut up into several distinct sections. In addition to the pit you'll notice huge tailing piles and ore dumps, old mine company buildings, abandoned rail lines, and several huge headframes where the miners were lowered into underground mines. Even though the last active mine shut down in 1975, there is still a huge mining presence in Bisbee.

The area of most interest to the visitor and where the stairways are located is old Bisbee on the north side of the pit. Old Bisbee is where copper and other minerals were first discovered in the 1870s and where full scale mining began in the 1880s.

That first discovery was made where two drainages come together just north of today's pit. The drainages now pass through a diversion channel to get around the pit. Old Bisbee sprouted up along the two drainages. Because of limited flat land at the bottom of the drainages, most of the houses had to be built on the slopes.

As the huge size of the mineral deposit became better known and developed, Bisbee prospered. By the early 20th century, Bisbee was making the transition from a mining boom town to a permanent community. Tents and shacks became cottages and homes. Temporary wooden buildings in the center of town became a tightly packed collection of substantial brick structures. As you

One of Bisbee's many headframes.

walk around you'll see that the bulk of the old commercial and public buildings were built approximately 100 years ago. By 1908 there was even a streetcar line connecting Bisbee to Warren. (Warren is south of the pit and is now one of the many sections of Bisbee.)

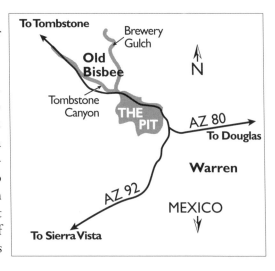

Because the slopes, where most of the people lived, were too steep for a street grid, very few streets were built. Most that were built more resemble an alley than a street. Many of them are very steep and narrow. Most of them are much easier to walk than to drive. As a result, old Bisbee developed with very little planning and houses popped up wherever someone could carve a flat enough terrace on the slope to build a home.

The organic nature of Bisbee's development is very much a part of the town's charm and funkiness. If you compare Bisbee to Warren (where the 1908 streetcar line went) you can see the difference between an organic community and a planned community.

Warren, located on flatter land than old Bisbee, was planned under the principles of the "City Beautiful" movement. Warren has spacious lots, wide roads, broad swaths of parkland, and a separate commercial district. Construction of Warren began in 1906. The ballpark built in Warren in 1909 is still used today.

With mining continuing to increase, there was a need to develop new areas to house the growing population. Certainly with overcrowding, a considerable amount of ramshackle housing, and poor sanitation in old Bisbee, Warren would have been an attractive alternative for many people living in Bisbee at that time.

But if you are visiting Bisbee as an outsider and drive around Warren today, you might say "that's interesting" or "oh that's nice" and then continue on your way without getting out of the car. But when you drive into old Bisbee, you'll have an "Oh Wow!" moment and be compelled to get out of the car and walk around.

There is nothing wrong with Warren. The houses seem nice and it may be a great place to live, but Warren just doesn't have the "it" factor of old Bisbee that sucks you in to spend more time. Instead the planned community of Warren has the feel of a very normal and quiet car-oriented neighborhood that you can find anywhere in the country.

The attraction of old Bisbee may be due to the fact that it has many of the elements that Jane Jacobs identified in her classic 1961 book, **The Death and Life of Great American Cities**, as to what makes a community vibrant, walkable, and exciting. Jacobs identified narrow streets with short blocks, a concentration of different types of activity, a diverse mixture of people, visually interesting buildings, and a combination of old and new buildings as key ingredients for a great walkable community. Old Bisbee has all of these.

Specifically, in old Bisbee the abundance of stairways plays the role of narrower streets and shorter blocks by providing pedestrian short cuts and multiple ways to reach any destination. Even though old Bisbee's buildings were built a long time ago, the individual decoration and expression added to them have made them fresh and gives them a sense of being both old and new.

Although old Bisbee is very walkable, it is not as walkable as a desirable neighborhood in a large city. This is because much of old Bisbee's commerce has evolved towards the needs of the visitor rather than that of the residents. If you want to eat at a restaurant, spend the night in a lodge, buy a work of art or a scented candle, old Bisbee has it. But with most of the everyday commerce of retail stores, medical services, schools, and governmental offices on the other side of the pit, you'll probably need to drive or take the bus to run an errand. In short, old Bisbee may be more walkable for the visitor than the resident.

If some of that everyday commerce were to come back to the north side of the pit, old Bisbee could become that ideal walkable community that many people desire. Fortunately, Bisbee does have bus service connecting the two sides of the pit for someone wanting to be relatively car free in old Bisbee.

Let's return to the organic nature of old Bisbee's hillside housing. Since Bisbee grew without many streets, the only way to reach most of the hillside houses was by foot. Over time a network of foot trails evolved to connect the houses on the hillside with the streets below. As one could expect, the trails became very slippery when it rained. To fix the problem, many of the trails were replaced by wooden stairways and sidewalks.

With the outbreak of World War I in Europe, the demand for copper grew and by 1916, a year before America entered the war, the population of the Bisbee area had grown to around 25,000. You might even read in some tourist literature that Bisbee was at that time the largest city between St. Louis and San Francisco. Even though this is an exaggeration, Bisbee was clearly a very important community.

It turns out that this was the high point of Bisbee's population. Increased mechanization and the start of open-pit mining began to reduce the number of people required to work the mines and Bisbee's population started declining. Some stability was achieved when the seat of Cochise County was moved from Tombstone to Bisbee in 1929. Regardless, the population was still trending down and the population today is around 5,500.

When the Great Depression came, Bisbee was hit hard. The price of copper plunged and took mining down with it. The New Deal programs of the Works Progress Administration (WPA) and the Civilian Conservation Corps (CCC) provided some relief.

The WPA paved dirt roads and replaced the wooden stairways of Bisbee with concrete. These are the stairways that you will be exploring and are the ones described in this guide. If you pay close attention, you'll see "USA / WPA" stamped into the concrete on many of the stairs you will be climbing. Many of the impressions are still as crisp and clear as if they were stamped into the concrete yesterday.

Both the WPA and CCC were involved in flood control projects in Bisbee. Although Bisbee has a semi-arid climate and the drainages normally run dry, there is rain and it can flood especially during summer thunderstorms. Uncontrolled runoff from heavy thunderstorms did cause problems in the early days of old Bisbee. Because of this, Bisbee built culverts very early in its history to divert runoff away from development. The WPA improved those culverts and added new ones where needed. You'll see these culverts as you walk around Bisbee.

The CCC assisted the flood control effort by building check dams and rock walls in the side canyons of the main drainages. They were built to let the rain water soak into the ground rather than rush into town. Some of these dams and walls were built with stacked stone, while others were built of rock mortared together with concrete. You'll see examples of both when you hike on the trails.

Because old Bisbee was more or less fully developed by the time of the Great Depression, new development has not wiped out the legacy of the WPA or the CCC. If you are a student of the New Deal or wish to celebrate the legacy of Franklin Delano Roosevelt, Bisbee is the place for you to explore.

With the coming of World War II, the price of copper recovered and the mines went back into full operation. Mining continued after the War and kept going until 1975 when Phelps Dodge Corporation, the owner of the mines, shut down the last mine.

Although full-scale mining has been gone for almost 40 years, there is still a limited amount of mining activity in Bisbee. Freeport-McMorRan, the successor company to Phelps Dodge, continues to recover copper from the piles of rock refuse and has an on-going project to remediate soil contaminated by the mining process. Much of the contamination came from smelters that were removed from Bisbee more than 100 years ago.

This is one of Bisbee's many soil remediation projects.

As you explore Bisbee, you can't help but to notice building lots bordered by yellow plastic sandbags and covered with straw. These are places where Freeport-McMorRan, or one of its contractors, recently removed the top soil and replaced it with new soil. You might even see a crew working on a soil remediation project when you walk around Bisbee.

When mining ended in 1975, Bisbee could have withered away and died like many other mining communities around the country. It could have dwindled to a shadow of what it once was by hanging on as a tourist attraction. Instead of living entirely on its past, Bisbee's beautiful setting, nice weather, strong "bones" of substantial commercial buildings, and the unbelievably low price of houses (some well less than $1000) attracted a new population of artistic and counter-culture types. Those bargains, unfortunately, are long gone.

The fresh perspective of the new residents brought in new life and energy to the town. Certainly Bisbee does have a past and provides plenty of opportunities to see that past. But it is what Bisbee is today that makes it so special. Wherever you turn in Bisbee, no matter how many times you walk the same route, you'll find something new, imaginative, interesting, and totally funky. And if only half of the notices posted on the utility poles and bulletin boards around town can be believed, there is no shortage of events to attend or things to do.

This new energy has not only made Bisbee a visitor destination; it has also attracted a more mainstream audience of people looking for a place to retire, or looking for a small town where they can work from home, or looking for a place to buy a second home. The city government of Bisbee believes that thirty percent of the houses in old Bisbee today are now second homes. In short, Bisbee has survived the end of mining and has made a new life for itself!

Like any place, Bisbee is not perfect and could stand to have a few more well-paying jobs. Despite any problems, Bisbee is a very open and welcoming community. It was the first town in Arizona to allow same-sex marriage, and its relaxed nature gives the town a laid back Key West feel where even the dogs seem relaxed. As I walked around with my dog, most of the local dogs wanted to play and run with him rather than snarl at him. It doesn't get better than Bisbee for taking a walk.

No matter how many times I walk around Bisbee, I have found it to be a peaceful and wonderful experience. There is always something new to discover, and there is always something textural to the experience. On one walk it was the fresh subtle scent of chinaberry trees in blossom and the crunch of millions of chinaberries under my feet. It seems that every stairway and pathway has several chinaberry trees. On another walk it was the faint licorice scent floating in the air from wild anise plants growing almost everywhere. A walk in Bisbee is always wonderful!

As You Walk Around Bisbee

As mentioned in the previous section, old Bisbee's stairway network came into being because the only place to build a house was on the hillside. As you glance around you'll notice that many of the hillside terraces where the houses were built are now vacant. These vacancies are a result of fires and selective abandonment over the years.

Some homes were abandoned when flatter building sites became available in places like nearby Warren. Others were abandoned as part of Bisbee's general population decline. But even with the many empty building sites, there are still plenty of hillside homes and still a definite need for stairways in Bisbee. And as you look around, imagine how congested Bisbee must have been 100 years ago when the empty building sites would have been full.

When you climb the stairs, you'll have chance to get a close look at many of the empty building sites. Some still have old concrete foundations or other remains in place. Some even have portions of an old concrete stairway. Can you imagine the effort it took to haul building material from the street down below to a building site high on the hillside?

As you continue walking you'll notice that many homeowners have cleaned up an adjacent empty terrace and turned it into an amazing sitting area with an incredible view. Many of the terraces have just the right decoration, shading, or exposure to be a perfect little paradise. In some places you might find a path leading to a wonderful place to be quiet. I cannot emphasize too much how you'll have

Can you imagine what it must have been like when every terrace had a house? That's the 115 OK Street stairway (# 11).

a sense of wandering from one personal Shangri-La to another when you walk in old Bisbee.

Most of the houses in Bisbee are very small and cozy. Some are absolute dollhouses that are a work of art in themselves. Some are less so; some much less so. In fact, the houses range all the way from

Bisbee has a long way to go before the funkiness is gentrified out of it.

abandoned and falling apart to perfect. No two houses are the same. And that, too, is part of the excitement and funkiness that makes walking around Bisbee such a special treat.

The diversity of housing ensures that all income groups have a shot at finding a place to live. This diversity is also part of Bisbee's charm. If every house were gentrified and the only cars on the street were BMWs, it would be boring and Bisbee would soon be on its way to becoming an exclusive haunt of the well-to-do.

In a town unique in so many ways, Bisbee is also unique in its way of numbering houses for street addresses. When you approach a stairway, you may notice that a house at street level has a normal street address such as, 151 Smith Street. As you start climbing the stairs, you may also notice that the house on the next terrace level will have an 'A' appended to its house number and have an address of 151A Smith Street. Each subsequent terrace level will then take on the next letter in the alphabet to become 151B, 151C… The highest house number identified in this guide ends with 'G', or seven terrace levels above the street. No wonder the U.S. Postal Service refuses to do house-to-house delivery in old Bisbee.

You may have read somewhere that Bisbee has 351 public stairways. That number was determined by counting the stairways shown on a map developed by a local engineer to identify every building lot and parcel of property in Bisbee. That map is no longer in print, and when it was available, it cost over $100. It was sold primarily to people in real estate and government.

The actual number of stairways in Bisbee may be higher than 351. With all the twists and turns and interconnecting network of stairways and sidewalks, it is difficult to find them all and also easy to count a stairway twice. If you add in stairways leading directly to someone's front door, or stairways leading to buildings that no longer exist, or stairways that branch off from larger stairways, or stairways now blocked off, the number of stairways quickly gets higher, and it may be impossible to come up with an accurate count. No matter what the actual count of stairways is, the density and number of stairways in old Bisbee is huge. You are never far from a stairway in old Bisbee.

I have learned that walking around Bisbee is like peeling off a layer of an onion. The only difference is that this onion has no end to its number of layers. Every time I go out, I find something new including new stairways or passageways to an area I had never seen before. With so many new discoveries, I keep feeling like an archaeologist uncovering a long-lost industrial-age community on every visit.

Andy Haratyk, the Operations Manager of the City of Bisbee's Public Works Department, told me that he tries to climb every stairway once a year but he can't because he keeps finding new stairways. Many people who I have met on my walks have told me the same thing. They keep peeling layers off the onion and their discoveries never end. And these are people who have lived in Bisbee for decades. It's so amazing to find so much in a town the size of Bisbee.

It may be impossible to produce a definitive count of or an absolute guide to all of Bisbee's stairs. To develop this guide I walked every street of old Bisbee, most of them several times, and climbed stairs wherever I found them. It is quite possible that I missed a path or sidewalk along a stairway that led to another stairway. So if you find a stairway that I missed, please let me know. A new discovery can always be added to a future edition.

The purpose of this guide is to help you explore Bisbee and to see all that it has to offer. To that end, this guide describes 82 stairways. They tend to be substantial stairways and have an average of 78 steps. The only thing left to be done is for you to get out there and start walking. It is the best way for you to see Bisbee and discover its funkiness.

All of the stairways described in this guide pass several terrace levels of houses and building lots or they are stairways that connect to other streets, sidewalks, or paths. Stairways that lead only to a single house or to a single terrace level of houses have not been included in this guide. Some smaller stairways are mentioned within the narrative but are not individually described; therefore, they are not included in the count of 82 stairways. If you believe that I omitted a stairway that should have been included in the count, please let me know.

There are also several sidewalk stairways mentioned

Sidewalk Stairway

The Bisbee Stairs   15

in the narrative. Only one of them is included in the stairway count. The sidewalk stairways are not individually described because they do not leave the road and take you away to one of Bisbee's hidden corners. This guide is about exploring as much as it is about climbing public stairways.

The stairways described in this guide are all important components of Bisbee's transportation infrastructure. In most cases, the only way to reach the houses along the stairways is by foot. This guidebook is organized as if you were taking a walk from the eastern edge of old Bisbee to the far western edge of town.

You can read this guide any way you prefer, of course, but I wrote it as a narrative. Rather than cherry-picking the guide for a specific street or stairway, it may be easier to read it in its entirety. You might find information within a particular stairway description that could prove useful elsewhere. Or you may read something in the narrative that you'll want to check out.

When you do start walking there is no need for you to follow the exact route of this narrative or to climb every stairway. There are plenty of maps in this guide to help you plot your own route. You may choose to start at one end of town, and go up and down stairways until you reach the other side of town. Another option is to follow a trail to the other end of town and then take stairways back.

Or you can follow the route of the Bisbee 1000. The Bisbee 1000 is an annual running race held in Bisbee every October. It includes running up nine stairways and has been called "the 5K that feels like a 10K". A map and more information on the Bisbee 1000 begins on the next page.

In addition to the stairways, this guide also briefly describes hiking trails and footpaths that can be found at the end of a street or a stairway. As you look around, you'll see plenty of open land above the developed areas of Bisbee. Much of that land is open to hiking and has well established trails.

Many of the abandoned terraces and building sites are now owned by the City of Bisbee. The City also owns much of the open land within the city limits above the terraces. If an area is not posted with no trespassing signs, it should be open to hiking. Much of the open mountain land beyond the city limits is also public land and open to hiking. If you do choose to hike, please remember that there are tracts of mining and private land where you cannot hike. If you come upon land posted with no trespassing signs, turn back. There are plenty of other places where you can hike.

Bisbee 1000

The Bisbee 1000, The Great Bisbee Stair Climb, is the only outdoor stair climb race of its caliber in the U.S. Always held on the third Saturday of October, the event is produced by Bisbee Vogue, Inc., a 501(c)3 whose mission is to create, facilitate, and support initiatives that promote the economic vitality, health, and wellness of citizens in Southern Arizona. It is one the biggest races in Arizona and attracts runners from around the country. It has even been featured in **Runners World**.

The 4.5 mile course includes nine sets of stairs that are connected by roads that take participants through some of the most scenic parts of Bisbee. The number of stairs participants climb is just over 1,000

© 2013 Tim Toms
Photo courtesy of Bisbee Vogue, Inc.

The Bisbee Stairs

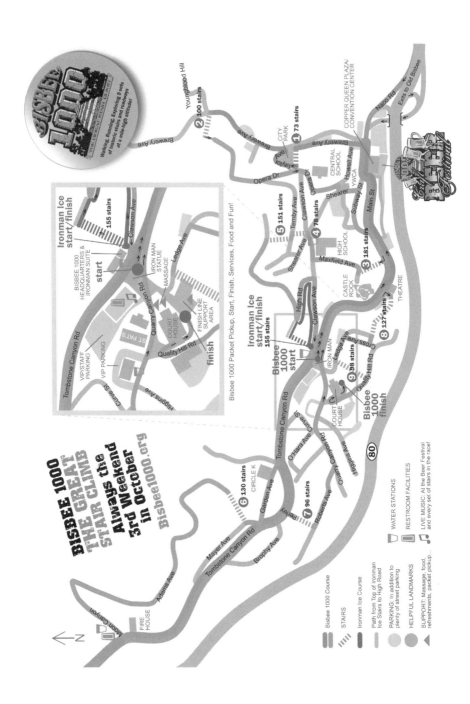

Photo courtesy of Bisbee Vogue, Inc.

One of the many Bisbee 1000 decorations created by Judy Perry

(1,094); thus the name. The race is the brainchild of long-time Bisbee resident Cynthia Conroy. She came up with the idea after reading a newspaper article in 1990 about the popularity of stair climbing machines at health and fitness clubs.

She thought "Why not climb real stairs?" and came up with the idea of a running race that features stairways along the route. To make the race a reality, she explored the streets of Bisbee to find the right stairs and the right route. The result was a figure-eight that touches every corner of Bisbee and includes nine of Bisbee's most charming stairways. You can recognize the stairways as they have all been decorated (or tattooed) by local artist Judy Perry. The route is a good way to get an overview of Bisbee.

The first Bisbee 1000 was held in October 1991 and attracted 200 runners. The race has grown in popularity every year. In 2013 more than 2000 runners participated. In order to keep the race better for the runners and a bit more manageable, the race is now capped at 1500 runners. You may see people running or walking the route to prepare for the race while you are exploring Bisbee.

In addition to the race, the Bisbee 1000 features the Ironman Ice Competition. This competition is named after the Iron Man statue which is where the race begins and which is across the street from the ice competition. The competition has become so popular that it now has its own day on the third Saturday of September.

The ice competition is a ¼-mile course that is done in a time trial fashion. The competition begins with participants securing a ten-pound block of ice with antique ice tongs. They then climb up a 155-step stairway (see page 58), run down a dirt path to a paved road, and then sprint downhill back to the starting point. Cynthia got the idea from a Three Stooges short (*An Ache in Every Stake*) where the Stooges had to carry a block of ice up a stairway in Los Angeles. By the time the Stooges reached the top of the stairway the block of ice had melted to the size of an ice cube.

If you would like to run in the Bisbee 1000 or participate in the Ice Competition please visit http://www.Bisbee1000.org/.

Section 2

Touring the Bisbee Stairways

As mentioned before, this guidebook is organized as a tour going from east to west. Because many of the stairs are interconnected and part of a network, I believe that this is the best way to give them some context.

As you explore the stairs, please keep in mind that some of the stairways are very steep or may be missing a handrail or may not be in perfect repair. If you look closely you'll also see that many stairways serve the same function as a street with gas, water, sewer, and electric utility lines running along the side and sometimes on top of the stairway. So please be careful and watch where you step to make sure you don't trip.

If you find yourself short of breath while climbing, don't despair or feel bad about taking a break. Some of the stairways are not only steep but very long. Bisbee's altitude of over 5000 feet also makes it easy to run out of breath. If you do take a break, it's a great opportunity to check out the view. You won't be disappointed no matter where you are.

As mentioned many times before, many of Bisbee's

Gas Line on a Stairway

homes can only be reached by stairs. Many of those houses are right on the stairs. So please be respectful of the fact that you might be passing within inches of someone's bedroom window and avoid being invasive.

You'll also see how the organic nature of Bisbee's development has caused many of the stair routes to make abrupt turns and jogs to the right or the left as they snake around a house on their way to the top. As a result many stairways may look like they're coming to an end when in fact they are just making a turn. Don't let your first impression discourage you from climbing a few more steps to make sure that the stairs have not come to an end. You might find another street or path right around the corner.

As for this guide, each stairway has an information line that includes: the stairway's reference number; the nearest street address; the number of steps; and whether the stairway has a stub ending or connects to something else. A description of the stairway, the setting, and what you might see along the way is below the information line. The description can range from one sentence to several paragraphs.

The stairway reference numbers begin with 1 and are in the order the stairway is described in the guide. The reference number is used to identify the stairway on the maps and for cross-referencing a stairway when it is mentioned in the narrative. The number will be shown in parentheses, such as (# 88). The stairway index on the next page also uses the reference number.

The step counts on the information line are based upon my personal count. Like any count, my count can be wrong. If you find a count to be seriously off, please let me know. Any inaccuracies can be fixed in a future edition.

For clarification, a stairway with a stub ending runs up the side of the hill and comes to an end without connecting to another street, sidewalk, or path. Many of the stub stairways are very long and have over 100 steps. Even though a stub ending requires that you take the stairway both up and down, many of them are worth exploring as they have so much for you to discover along the way.

Bisbee Stairway Index

Ref. #	Stairway	Steps	Bisbee 1000	Type	Page
1	120 Naco Road (east)	65		Stub	30
2	120 Naco Road (west)	109		Stub	30
3	11 OK Street	57		Stub	31
4	29 OK Street	122		Stub	32
5	45 OK Street	29		Connects	33
6	55A OK Street (south)	71		Stub	33
7	55A OK Street (north)	44		Stub	34
8	75A OK Street	88		Connects	34
9	69 OK Street	30		Connects	34
10	101 OK Street	114		Connects	36
11	115 OK Street	108		Connects	36
12	135 OK Street	95		Stub	37
13	139 OK Street	54		Stub	37
14	149 OK Street	80		Stub	37
15	153 OK Street	38		Stub	38
16	215 Brewery Ave. (north)	122		Connects	39
17	215 Brewery Ave. (south)	56		Connects	40
18	217B Brewery Ave. (south)	42		Connects	40
19	217B Brewery Ave. (north)	66		Connects	40
20	203 Brewery Avenue	60		Connects	41
21	147 Brewery Avenue	91		Connects	41
22	113 Brewery Avenue	68		Connects	42
23	65 Brewery Avenue	18		Connects	42
24	41 Brewery Avenue	46		Connects	43
25	15 Brewery Avenue	30		Connects	43
26	24 Brewery Avenue	53		Connects	43
27	Central School Alley	16		Connects	44
28	City Park	73	Stairway # 1	Connects	44
29	Walsh Avenue Stairway	96		Connects	44
30	120 Brewery Avenue	75		Connects	45
31	202 Brewery Avenue	160	Stairway # 2	Connects	45
32	216 Brewery Avenue	80		Connects	46
33	232 Opera Drive	100		Stub	47
34	226 Opera Drive	45		Stub	48
35	138 Upper Opera Drive	109		Stub	49
36	200 Upper Opera Drive	108		Connects	50
37	137 Opera Drive	116		Connects	50
38	1B Temby Avenue	75		Connects	52
39	7A Temby Avenue	95		Connects	52
40	12 Temby Avenue	65		Connects	53

The Bisbee Stairs

Ref. #	Stairway	Steps	Bisbee 1000	Type	Page
41	21 Temby Avenue	117		Connects	53
42	31 Temby Avenue	75	Stairway # 4	Connects	53
43	37 Temby Avenue	151	Stairway # 5	Connects	54
44	45 Temby Avenue	54		Stub	55
45	End of Hunt Avenue Stairway	72		Stub	55
46	85 Shearer Avenue	80		Connects	56
47	68 High Road	77		Connects	56
48	129 High Road	50		Stub	57
49	Ironman Ice Stairs	155		Connects	58
50	127 Clawson Avenue	51		Stub	58
51	Quality Hill Walk	88	Stairway # 9	Connects	59
52	County Admin Building (east)	58		Connects	60
53	186 Ledge Avenue	93		Connects	60
54	114 Ledge Avenue	127	Stairway # 8	Connects	61
55	186 Quality Hill Road	28		Connects	62
56	81 Main Street	181	Stairway # 3	Connects	62
57	13 Maxfield Avenue	50		Stub	63
58	59C Maxfield Avenue	141		Connects	65
59	Angius Stairs	46		Connects	67
60	19 Clawson Avenue	44		Stub	67
61	9 Clawson Avenue	26		Connects	67
62	203 Tombstone Canyon Rd.	67		Stub	68
63	225 Tombstone Canyon Rd.	92		Stub	69
64	317 Tombstone Canyon Rd.	39		Connects	69
65	Bus Stop Stairs	30		Connects	69
66	Perley Street Stairs	96	Stairway # 7	Connects	70
67	Evans Street Stairs	62		Stub	71
68	Brophy Sidewalk Stairway	105		Stub	71
69	505 Brophy Avenue	90		Connects	72
70	15 Art Avenue	164		Connects	73
71	29 Art Avenue	144		Connects	74
72	503 Mayer Avenue	136	Stairway # 6	Connects	75
73	511 Mayer Avenue	81		Stub	76
74	534 Tombstone Canyon Rd.	60		Stub	76
75	Gladys Avenue Stairway	143		Connects	77
76	5 Moon Canyon	49		Stub	78
77	643 Tombstone Canyon Rd.	64		Stub	78
78	729 Tombstone Canyon Rd.	56		Connects	78
79	735 Tombstone Canyon Rd.	76		Connects	79
80	734 Gentry Avenue	41		Connects	80
81	826 Sims Road	39		Connects	80
82	Pump House Stairway	111		Connects	80

BISBEE STAIRWAY MAPS

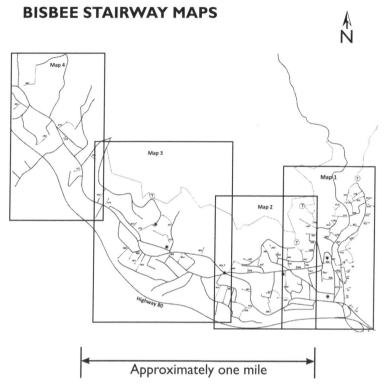

Approximately one mile

- Stairways are shown as arrows; the arrowhead points uphill
- The "T" in the circle is a trailhead
- The solid dot with a circle is a landmark
- dash lines are trails

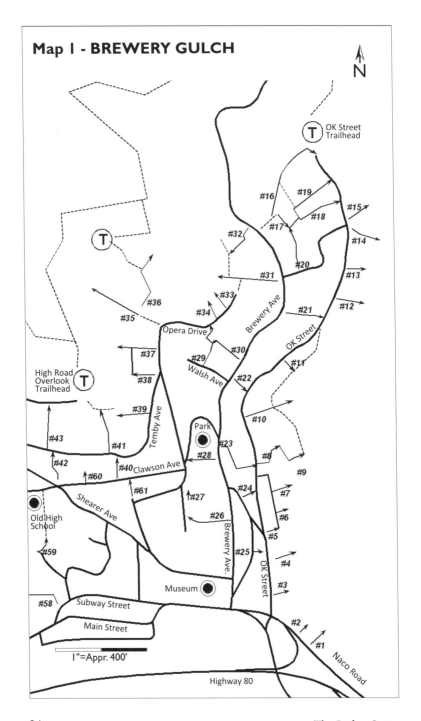

Map 2 - CENTRAL COMMERCIAL DISTRICT

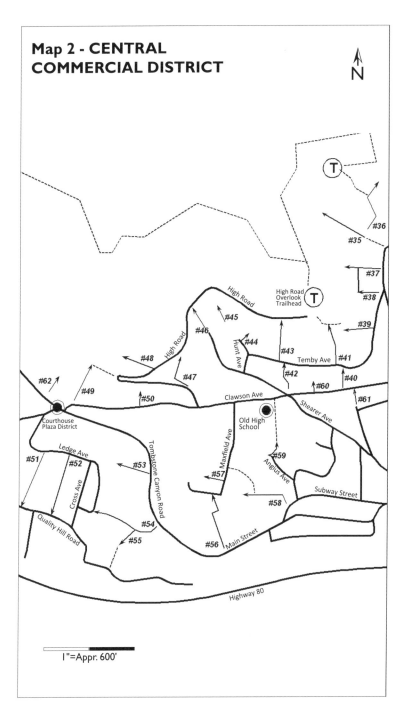

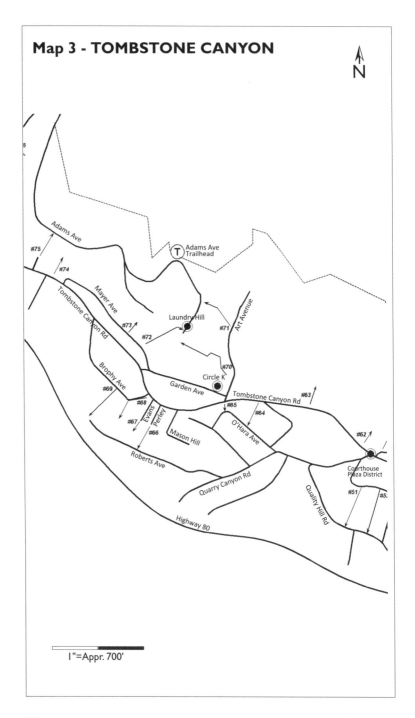

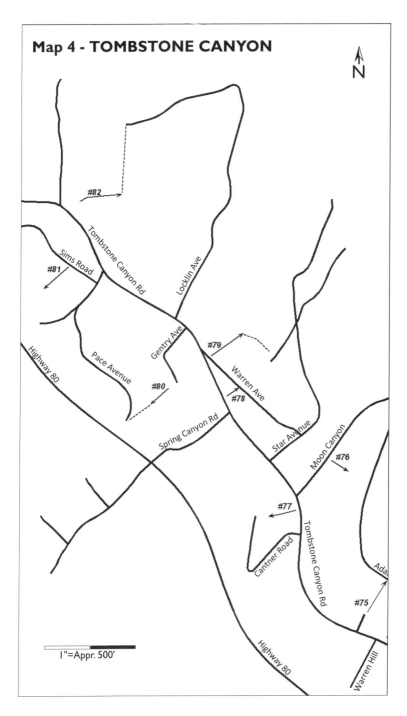

The Tour Begins on Naco Road

As you enter old Bisbee from the east to begin the tour, you'll pass through the inside edge of the old open-pit mine and will find Naco Road right after the pit. The first two stairways are on the right-hand side of Naco Road at the base of Chihuahua Hill. Depending on your angle of vision, you'll be able to see a huge "B" hovering above old Bisbee on the side of Chihuahua Hill.

The two Naco Road stairways are located on either side of an old commercial building at 120 Naco. It is next door to the former City Hall built in 1918.

1. 120 Naco Road (east); 65 steps; Stub ending

    This stairway is immediately to the right of the 120 Naco building (on the east side) and has a stairway chairlift that has seen better days. The stairs lead to several eclectic homes perched on the side of the hill and comes to an end at a no trespassing sign.

2. 120 Naco Road (west); 109 steps; Stub ending

    You'll find this stairway on the other side of the 120 Naco building. It is wedged between the 120 building and the old City Hall. A plaque identifying the 120 Naco building as being listed in National Register is immediately to the right of the stairs. At the base of the stairs, you can clearly see USA / WPA stamped into the concrete. You will see USA / WPA stamped into the concrete throughout Bisbee.

    Once the stairway clears the 120 Naco building it curves around to reach different terrace levels of homes. One of the homes near the top has an address of 11B OK Street. That home also has access to another stairway coming off of OK Street. The stairs end at a new garage built on a new driveway coming up from Naco Road.

    If you look toward the top of Chihuahua Hill you'll see that there are more terrace levels and home sites above you. At one time there were probably more trails and stairs to reach them. If you look back across Bisbee, you'll have an excellent view of downtown.

Orienting Yourself for the Remainder of the Tour

As you walk past the old City Hall, you'll soon come to OK Street. If you look closely, across the street, you'll see a very short stretch of railroad tracks in the pavement from the old streetcar line that once ran to Warren. (The last streetcar ran in 1928.) The next street over to the west is Brewery Avenue. This is the general area where the two drainages of old Bisbee come together.

The drainage heading north, to your right, is Brewery Gulch. It eventually becomes Zacatecas Canyon after it passes through the developed area of Bisbee. The drainage coming in from the west, in front of you, is Tombstone Canyon. The commercial center of old Bisbee is also in front of you.

For exploring purposes, old Bisbee can be divided into three sections: Brewery Gulch, the commercial center, and Tombstone Canyon beyond the commercial center. This tour will explore Brewery Gulch first by making a right-hand turn on to OK Street.

OK Street

OK Street is the easternmost north and south running street of old Bisbee. It is on a bench of Chihuahua Hill on the east slope of Brewery Gulch. OK Street runs above and generally parallel to Brewery Avenue at the bottom of Brewery Gulch.

As you go north on OK Street, the tour will explore the stairways going uphill to your right. The tour will cover the stairs on your left, going downhill to Brewery Avenue, when it goes along Brewery Avenue. Although OK Street is a two-way road, it is very narrow and in many places it only has one lane where it is impossible for two approaching cars to pass each other. Like most streets in Bisbee, OK Street is much easier to walk than to drive.

You'll run into your first stairway on OK Street almost immediately at 11 OK Street.

3. 11 OK Street; 57 steps; Stub ending

   Immediately south of the Jail House Inn you'll see a short brick walkway wedged between two buildings that leads to an old steel door. When I first saw the walkway, I thought that it ended at the steel door. But when I walked towards the door I discovered a stairway off to left leading to a little paradise of palm trees and several houses.

4. 29 OK Street (Pythian Apartments); 122 steps; Stub ending

This steep stairway runs up the south side of the Pythian apartment building. Per the date on the old clock tower and the name on the front, the building was built in 1904 as a Pythian Castle for the Knights of Pythias. This was one of the many fraternal orders located in Bisbee during its heyday. The clock tower no longer has a clock.

One of the opportunities of wandering around a town like Bisbee is to see how much the world has changed. One hundred plus years ago a man of a certain stature was expected to join a fraternal lodge like the Knights of Pythias. Today fraternal lodges are in steep decline and many people today wouldn't even recognize the name Knights of Pythias. Who knows what from today will seem quaint and unrecognizable one hundred years from now?

The stairway leads to a small sidewalk. To the left there is a gated stairway leading to a single house. To the right there is a very steep stairway going uphill.

The stairs pass several old foundations and terrace levels that once held houses. Because these stairs are rarely used, they are in very poor repair. The City of Bisbee does not have sufficient funds to maintain stairs that no longer have houses.

Across the street from the Pythian Building is a different stairway (# 25) going down to Brewery Avenue.

5. 45 OK Street (Hotel Lamore); 29 steps; Connects to a sidewalk above the hotel

   The hotel building was built in 1912 as miners' lodging. The stairway is immediately south of the building and leads to a sidewalk above the building. If you make a right-hand turn on the sidewalk you can climb 38 more steps to reach a house.

   If you turn left on the sidewalk you'll be above and behind the Hotel Lamore. If you continue north on the sidewalk you'll pass behind the El Dorado Suites Hotel. The El Dorado building was built in 1914 as a miners' boardinghouse. On the uphill side of the sidewalk there is an old apartment building (55A OK Street) built in 1905. The 55A apartment building has stairways (#'s 6 & 7) on either side of it.

   Hard to believe that this sidewalk/alley at 69 OK Street leads to several stairways.

   If you look at a survey map from 1905, this particular sidewalk was considered to be a city street. Many of the stairways, paths, and sidewalks were planned as streets. They are in effect "paper streets" and are perfect places for wandering.

   If you continue walking on this sidewalk, you'll rejoin OK Street further north at 69 OK. If you were to pass the opening at 69 OK while walking along OK Street, you would never realize that the small alley-like walk to your side led to houses and stairways.

6. 55A OK Street (south); 71 steps; Stub ending

   These stairs are immediately south of the 55A apartment building and lead to three terrace levels of houses. The end of this stairway is directly below the 'B' on Chihuahua Hill. There are two more terrace levels of old foundations above the stairway. There are also some very faint paths beyond the stairway, but they may be more trouble than they are worth to hike.

7. 55A OK Street (north); 44 steps; Stub ending

   This stairway is immediately north of the 55A apartment building and follows a drainage in a concrete culvert going up the side of the hill. The stairs lead to houses and abandoned building lots.

8. 75A OK Street; 88 steps; Stub ending and Connects to a trail

   This stairway curves up from OK Street and passes three terrace levels of houses and ends at a gate with a no trespassing sign. There are several abandoned building lots above and beyond the gate.

   When you reach the top there will be another gate to your right. This gate does not have a no trespassing sign. The gate opens on to a path that leads to another stairway (#9) that is above 69 OK Street.

   There is another stairway (#23) across the street from the bottom of the 75A OK stairway going down to Brewery Avenue.

9. 69 OK Street; 30 steps; Connects to a trail

   This stairway is a perfect example of how Bisbee can be a maze and an explorer's delight. When you see the no trespassing sign at the end of the 75A stairway (#8), your first reaction is to turn back. But if you persist by going through the gate to the right and

These are the hand-made steps leading to the cave.

walking down the path, you will find a set of stairs and be well rewarded.

When you get to the 30th step of the stairway, you will be just below the address of 69E OK Street (five terraces above OK Street) and will see some hand-made steps going off to your left. If you follow the steps you'll reach a terrace level with a small cave dug into the side of the mountain. The cave is plenty big enough for four or five people to stand inside it. Within the cave is a wonderful Buddhist shrine.

The shrine was built by a neighbor who lives on the 69 OK stairway that we just climbed. According to another neighbor, the builder of the shrine welcomes visitors.

If you continue up the hand-made steps to the next terrace level you will find a path heading north that crosses the 101 OK Street and the 115 OK Street stairways (#'s 10 & 11). The path

This is the cave with the shrine.

will eventually rejoin OK Street further north at 129 OK. There you will find a short eight-step stairway to take you down to street level.

10. 101 OK Street; 114 steps; Stub ending and Connects to a trail

This stairway passes three terrace levels of houses and building lots before coming to an end at the dirt and gravel path mentioned in the 69 OK Street stairway (# 9) description. If you look carefully, you can see remains of stairs continuing further up the hill to now empty terrace levels. When you turn right (heading south), you'll soon be above Bisbee and have some incredible views of downtown for taking a picture. You'll also pass some hand-made steps that lead to a house above the path. If you look down while walking you'll see several personal paradises and many great examples of folk art. If you keep walking you'll soon reach the 69 OK Street stairway (# 9) and its associated Buddhist shrine.

If you turn left on the path (heading north), you'll cross the 115 OK stairway (#11) and eventually reach the small eight-step stairway to rejoin OK Street at 129 OK.

There is another stairway (#22) across the street from the bottom of the 101 OK stairway going down to Brewery Avenue.

11. 115 OK Street; 108 steps; Stub ending and Connects to a trail

(Left) This is the eight-step stairway at 129 OK Street that leads to the path that connects to three stairways (#'s 9, 10, & 11)

This stairway is very steep and similar to the 101 OK stairway (# 10). The path connecting the 101 OK and 69 OK stairways (#'s 10 & 9) to 129 OK Street is at the 60th step. The stairway continues going up to empty terrace levels and abandoned building lots above the path.

12. 135 OK Street; 95 steps; Stub ending

This stairway leads to houses and passes several terrace levels and abandoned building lots. On your way up, you'll pass another set of stairs leading off to the left to a colorful gingerbread-like house. The stairway ends at a shaded terrace with an enclosed water catchment basin.

The 135 OK Street stairway (# 12) continues past the gingerbread-like house.

13. 139 OK Street; 54 steps; Stub ending

This stairway is very cracked and twisted and is not worth climbing. The stairs once went higher but now become unusable after 54 steps.

As you continue walking north, you'll reach the intersection of OK Street and Youngblood Hill Road. OK Street continues north to a dead end. Youngblood Hill Road goes down the hill to Brewery Avenue. The concrete drainage ditch on the side of Youngblood Hill Road was built by the WPA during the Great Depression as a flood control project.

There is a drainage going uphill from the intersection. There are also stairways going uphill on each side of the drainage.

14. 149 OK Street; 80 steps; Stub ending

This stairway is south of the drainage and leads to a house and several abandoned building lots.

15. 153 OK Street; 38 steps; Stub ending

> This stairway is north of the drainage and begins as a ramp that is a continuation of Youngblood Hill Road. The ramp eventually becomes a stairway with a faded USA / WPA stamped into the concrete that leads to houses. The Emory oaks and chinaberry trees growing along the drainage provide considerable shade and contribute to the stairway's Shangri-La feel.

As you continue north, OK Street will come to an end at 217 and 227 OK Street. You'll also see two stairways (#'s 18 & 19) going down to Brewery Avenue on your left before you reach the end of OK Street. At the end of OK Street you'll see another stairway (# 16) on the left going down to Brewery Avenue. It is next to the fire hydrant. On the right you'll see a concrete driveway leading up to a gate for 238 OK Street.

There is an unmarked trailhead at the end of the driveway. It's on the right-hand side just before the gate. The trail leads to the cross and several shrines at the top of Youngblood Hill. You may have noticed the cross when you were walking up OK Street. A branch of the trail continues beyond Youngblood Hill to some wonderful high-desert landscape above the northern reaches of Brewery Gulch and Zacatecas Canyon. (For more information, see *Hikes from the End of OK Street* on page 85).

Stairways Going Uphill from Brewery Avenue towards OK Street (to the east)

The stairway tour continues by taking the stairway (# 16) at the end of OK Street (at the fire hydrant between 217 and 227 OK Street) down to 215 Brewery Avenue. You will reach Brewery just north of Mimosa Market.

To continue the tour you'll be turning left (toward the south) at the bottom of the stairs. The tour will go south on Brewery Avenue to Naco Road and examine the stairs going uphill from Brewery Avenue to OK Street. When you reach Naco Road, you'll return on Brewery Avenue to cover the stairs going uphill on the other side of the street.

According to locals this is what's left of Bisbee's "red light" district

If you to turn right on Brewery Avenue (heading north) you can, according to locals, find the remains of Bisbee's "red light" district from a hundred years ago. It's just beyond where the road bends and across the street from 241 Brewery Avenue. You'll recognize the location by several short five-step stairways going up to a now empty building lot. If you continue heading north, the pavement will end and the road will narrow as it heads up Zacatecas Canyon. You will pass some stairways along the way but they only lead to a single terrace level of homes and abandoned building lots.

To resume the stairway tour, you'll turn around and head back toward the Mimosa Market at 215 Brewery Avenue.

16. 215 Brewery Avenue (north); 122 steps; Connects to 217 OK Street

> This is the stairway that you took down from the end of OK Street. It is an important connector from Brewery Avenue to the north end of OK Street and is the best way to reach the trailhead at the end of OK Street.
>
> The stairway begins as a sidewalk and then curves along a drainage at a gentle grade. The middle portion of the stairway is a sidewalk. Unfortunately, you'll probably notice trash along the way and see that parts of the stairway need repairs. Regardless of

the stairs' appearance, this stairway is very usable. As an added bonus Mimosa Market is at the bottom of the stairs for getting a snack.

17. 215 Brewery Avenue (south); 56 steps; Connects to a sidewalk above Brewery Avenue

    This stairway is immediately behind Mimosa Market and goes up and off to the right. It leads to a sidewalk with several houses overlooking Brewery Avenue down below. The sidewalk ends at the 203 Brewery stairway (#20) that leads down to the intersection of Youngblood Hill Road and Brewery Avenue.

    When you reach the top of the stairs, look closely at the railing on your left. You'll see a gap in the railing and the beginning of a path right after you reach the top of the stairs at 217B Brewery Avenue. If you follow the path around the house, you'll find another stairway (# 18).

18. 217B Brewery Avenue (south); 42 steps; Connects to 205 OK Street

    This stairway begins behind 217B Brewery. After climbing 13 steps you'll see another stairway (# 19), 217B Brewery (north), going to the left. But if you jog to the right you'll see that the stairs continue up along a drainage to 205 OK Street. These steps are almost spooky as they are steep and dark. As an added bonus, you'll need to duck under a sewer pipe before you reach the top.

19. 217B Brewery Avenue (north); 66 steps; Connects to 207 OK Street

    When I first saw these stairs from OK Street, I thought that they only went down to one house. But when I took another look, I noticed that there was another flight of steps in front of the house and began exploring.

    The bottom of this stairway begins at the 13th step of the 217B Brewery (south) stairway (# 18). The first 10-step flight of these stairs leads to a sidewalk with USA / WPA stamped into the concrete. The sidewalk leads to another flight of stairs going up. The sidewalk also continues past the flight of stairs (see the next paragraph). Continuing up the stairway, it passes a level of houses and reaches a small empty lot. A few feet away there is another flight of stairs going up to 207 OK Street.

If you stay on the sidewalk, you'll find that it soon becomes a narrow ledge without a railing and with a steep drop to the left. After the sidewalk clears the ledge it becomes a path that leads to the 215 Brewery (north) stairway (# 16). From there you can take the stairs up to OK Street or down to Brewery Avenue.

20. 203 Brewery Avenue; 60 steps; Connects to a sidewalk above Brewery Avenue

The entrance to this stairway is actually on the east side of Youngblood Hill Road; one house in from Brewery Avenue. The stairway passes along the side of the historic Muheim House before reaching the sidewalk. The Muheim House is sometimes open as a museum and can be reached from the sidewalk. The sidewalk continues to the path that leads to the 217B Brewery stairways (#'s 18 & 19) and to the 215 Brewery (south) stairway (#17).

21. 147 Brewery Avenue; 91 steps; Connects to 125/149 OK Street

You'll pass this house on the 147 Brewery stairway (# 21).

The Bisbee Stairs

This stairway begins as a sidewalk and then becomes a ramp behind the 147 Brewery building. The stairway is at the end of the ramp. The stairway has a lower section and upper section connected by a shaded sidewalk. There is a very nice house with a great yard along the sidewalk.

The stairway ends at OK Street across from the eight-step stairway that goes up to the footpath that leads to the 115, 101, and 69 OK stairways (#'s 11, 10, & 9). This is the path that takes you to the Buddhist cave shrine. (See stairway # 9 for a description.)

22. 113 Brewery Avenue (across from Walsh Street); 68 steps; Connects to 101 OK Street

This stairway has two sections: 39 very steep metal steps at the top and 29 concrete steps at the bottom. This stairway is across the street from the steps at 101 OK Street (#10). If you're looking for a longer climb you can combine the 68 steps of this stairway with the 114 steps of the 101 OK Street stairway (# 10) across the street for a total of 182 steps.

23. 65 Brewery Avenue; 18 steps; Connects to 75A OK Street

This short stairway begins as a path through the parking area on the north side of the 65 Brewery building. The path becomes a brick alley behind the building. The brick alley narrows to a path and turns left to reach the stairway. If you combine the 18 steps of this stairway with the 88 steps of the stairway (# 8) across the street at 75A OK you would have a 106 step stairway. You can add another 30 steps to your climb by including the 69 OK stairway (# 9).

The brick alley behind 65 Brewery Avenue leads to the hidden 65 Brewery stairway (# 23).

24. 41 Brewery Avenue; 46 steps; Connects to 55 OK Street

    This stairway is on the south side of the 41 Brewery building and ends directly across the street from the El Dorado Suites Hotel on OK Street. The stairway provides a connection for the hotel to the bars and restaurants on Brewery Avenue. The St. Elmo bar on Brewery Avenue is directly across the street from the bottom of the stairway. St. Elmo is advertised as the oldest bar (since 1902) in Bisbee.

25. 15 Brewery Avenue; 30 steps; Connects to 29 OK Street

    This metal stairway is behind and to the east of the Muheim Block building. You'll recognize the Muheim Block as the building with the word "Brewery" above the door and 1905 at the top. You can reach the stairway by following the sidewalk in front of the building. The sidewalk crosses an alley-like street to reach the stairway. The stairs go up to the Pythian Apartment building.

This is the last of the stairways connecting Brewery Avenue to OK Street. You are now very close to where you started at OK Street and Naco Road. It's now time to start working the other side of Brewery Avenue.

Stairways Going Uphill from Brewery Avenue towards Opera Drive (to the west)

The tour continues from here and works its way back towards 215 Brewery. The intersection of Brewery Avenue and Naco Road is on the east side of the central commercial area and has several bars, stores, and restaurants. As you walk north, keep an eye open for incredible folk art and eclectic decorations. The first stairway is on your left between two storefronts.

26. 24 Brewery Avenue; 53 steps; Connects to an alley behind old Central School

    This stairway is identified on old survey maps as School Alley. It begins between two storefronts at 24 and 26 Brewery and is a passageway with a gentle grade leading to several houses behind the stores. It ends at an alley behind old Central School. The school is now an art center. If you turn right when you reach the alley, you'll find a small stairway at the end of the alley leading to Opera Drive.

One of the houses you'll pass on your way to the old Central School.

27. Central School Alley; 16 steps; Connects to Opera Drive

This stairway connects the alley behind old Central School to Opera Drive. This stairway combined with the 24 Brewery Avenue stairway (#26) is a good short cut to the stores and restaurants at Brewery Avenue and Naco Road.

28. City Park; 73 steps; Connects to the junction of Opera Drive and Taylor Avenue

This is Stairway # 1 of the Bisbee 1000. It follows the south edge of City Park next to the band shell. The band shell happens to have great acoustics. One time while walking on the path at the top of the 101 OK Street stairway (# 10), I could hear someone singing in the band shell way down below as if they were standing right next to me.

City Park was built in 1916 on what had been the city cemetery. There is a smaller 21-step stairway, that is not included in the description of stairways, on the north side of the park.

29. Walsh Avenue Stairway; 96 steps; Connects to 223 Opera Drive

This stairway begins in the middle of several vacant lots just west of Brewery Avenue. It has several sidewalk portions and makes two 90-degree turns to reach Opera Drive. After the first turn there is a path that leads to a parking area at a terrace level below Opera Drive and a level above Brewery. The stairway

(# 22) at 113 Brewery Avenue going up to OK Street is across the street from Walsh.

When you reach the top of the stairway at Opera Drive, you will see an incredible decorated retaining wall across the street with amazing representations of native Alaskan art and other surprises. This is one of many many funky folk art displays that can keep you wandering in Bisbee for days. The next house over has covered their retaining wall with decorative glass items. The folk art never stops.

This is just a small portion of the wall at the top of the steps.

30. 120 Brewery Avenue; 75 steps; Connects to one of the sidewalks on the Walsh steps

    The USA / WPA stamp in the concrete is readily noticeable on this stairway. This stairway combined with the Walsh Avenue steps forms a network of stairs, sidewalks, and paths that connects several levels of houses and abandoned building lots with Brewery Avenue down below and Opera Drive up above.

31. 202 Brewery Avenue (across from Youngblood Hill Road); 160 steps; Stub ending and Connects to a path that leads to Opera Drive and also Connects to a sidewalk that leads to the 216 Brewery stairway (# 32)

    The first 100 steps of this stairway is Stairway #2 of the Bisbee 1000. The Bisbee 1000 makes a left-hand turn at the 100th step and heads down the path to Opera Drive. You'll recognize the path by the painting of a runner on the wall in front of you. There is also a small shrine to the Virgin Mary on your left a few steps before you reach the path to Opera Drive.

The stairway continues up beyond the path for 60 more steps to a stub ending. Seventeen steps above the Opera Drive path, behind a terrace level of houses, you'll see a sidewalk/path going off to the right. The sidewalk eventually connects to the stairway (# 32) at 216 Brewery Avenue. It's almost like a maze to get there from here. Can you imagine giving someone directions on how to reach your home if you lived here?

Follow the path to Opera Drive.

32. 216 Brewery Avenue (across the street and a bit north of Mimosa Market); 80 steps; Connects to an unnamed alley-like spur off of Brewery Avenue and Connects to a sidewalk that leads to the 202 Brewery stairway (# 31)

This stairway begins between 216 and 222 Brewery Avenue. When you look at the stairs from the street you would expect the stairway to go up only to the first house. But when you climb them you'll find a maze of turns and jogs to reach three levels of houses. Along the way you'll see a spectacular garden with amazing statues.

Keep following the stairs up, you'll be glad you did.

46   *The Bisbee Stairs*

You'll pass this incredible garden along the way.

At the top you'll reach a path and a sidewalk. The path going off to the right leads to an alley-like spur of Brewery Avenue. If you're adventurous, you can find a foot path leading up from the alley to a couple of houses and abandoned building lots. The sidewalk to the left connects to the 202 Brewery stairway (# 31).

This is the end of the stairways along Brewery Avenue. As mentioned earlier, the remaining stairways along Brewery Avenue lead only to a single terrace level of homes and abandoned building lots. The tour will now start exploring the streets to the west of and above Brewery Avenue. The tour will begin with Opera Drive.

Stairways along Opera Drive

This part of the tour begins where Opera Drive is joined by the path from the 202 Brewery Avenue stairway (# 31). This is actually the end of one of Opera Drive's branches so you can proceed straight ahead. You will soon find a stairway going uphill off to your right at 232 Opera Drive.

33. 232 Opera Drive; 100 steps; Stub ending

    USA / WPA is predominantly stamped into the concrete. If you've ever wanted to walk with an angel, this is your stairway.

Look up to the right and you'll see one.

As you walk around, you may have been wondering about the yellow plastic sandbags and straw spread around the ground. These are building lots where the mining company Freeport-McMorRan has performed soil reme-

diation by removing the top soil and replacing it with new soil. You'll see several examples of soil remediation on this stairway.

34. 226 Opera Drive; 45 steps; Stub ending

This stairway leads to houses and abandoned building lots. The stairway also crosses a short path leading back to the nearby 232 Opera Drive stairway (# 33).

You'll pass this wall as you walk along Opera Drive.

As you continue along Opera Drive the road will curve to the right. If you look across the street, you can see the Walsh Avenue stairway (# 29) going down. As you continue walking, you'll pass the amazing retaining walls mentioned in the Walsh Avenue stairway (# 29) description and will soon reach a road junction.

Opera Drive goes off to the left while Upper Opera Drive is a short spur that goes straight ahead and a bit to the right. The tour will take a few moments to check out Upper Opera. Very soon you'll see a set of stairs going off to the left at 138 Upper Opera.

35. 138 Upper Opera Drive; 109 steps; Stub ending

> This stairway has a nice gentle grade as it follows a drainage with plenty of shade up the hill. This is a very pleasant walk with a lot to see along the way. You will pass houses, abandoned building lots, sidewalks and stairs that no longer connect to houses, and evidence of soil remediation projects.
>
> The stairway ends at 138F Upper Opera. As mentioned earlier, the letter in an address represents the terrace level of a house. The letter F would be the sixth terrace level. A path leading to old building foundations and at least two more terrace levels continues beyond the end of the stairway. During Bisbee's heyday there would have been no less than eight levels of houses connected to the world by this stairway.

You'll see these old foundations at the top of the stairway.

The Bisbee Stairs

36. 200 Upper Opera Drive; 108 steps; Stub ending and Connects to a trailhead

   Because the houses along this stairway have access to the road, these stairs are not in the best of repair. You do cross an interesting USA / WPA concrete culvert bridge to reach the stairs, and you can get some great views from the top of the stairway.

   Instead of climbing the final flight of stairs, you can follow the dirt walkway to the road and then walk up the steep roadway to a trailhead. The trailhead is below the old water storage tank that you can see on the side of the hill in front of you. There you'll find a footpath going up a no longer usable roadway or mule path.

   The GPS coordinates for the trailhead are: N 31°26'47.0"; W 109°54'56.8"

   If you follow the trail, you'll reach another trail in less than 500 feet. It is the trail going from the High Road Overlook to Zacatecas Canyon. There's even a faded sign painted on the rock showing you the direction to Laundry Hill. The trails to Laundry Hill and to Zacatecas Canyon are described in greater detail in *Hikes from the High Road Overlook* on page 89.

   There are other trails in the area that lead to some great overlooks and sitting areas.

After visiting Upper Opera Drive, it's time to turn around and return to Opera Drive. You'll soon find another stairway at 137 Opera Drive.

37. 137 Opera Drive; 116 steps; Stub ending and Connects to a sidewalk leading to the 1B Temby stairway (# 38)

   This stairway is easy to miss. With its overhanging chinaberry trees, the base of the stairway looks like a dark shaded opening in the concrete retaining wall. It almost looks like you shouldn't enter, but you can; it's a public stairway. Adding to the eeriness is a large thick piece of iron hanging next to the retaining wall at the bottom of the stairway. If you tap the iron against the retaining wall, it will sound like a deep trembling gong. This is

Petey waiting to climb the 137 Opera stairway (# 37).

another of many reasons why it's so cool to walk around Bisbee.

The stairs go straight up the hillside. At the 69th step, above the B terrace level, there is a sidewalk going off to the left. (The tour will return to the sidewalk after you finish climbing to the top.) The stairs continue going up and end at the D terrace level. There are some local trails at the end of the stairs that are not very usable.

If you go back to the 69th step and follow the sidewalk, you'll pass several houses and see USA / WPA stamped into the concrete. The sidewalk ends at the top of the 1B Temby stairway (# 38).

If you return to Opera Drive and continue south, you'll pass a gated stairway at 132 Opera. Although you can't

The Bisbee Stairs   51

climb the stairs, you can still admire the great artwork around the opening. There is a split in the road just in front of you. Opera Drive veers to the left and goes downhill to the center of town. Temby Avenue veers to the right and goes uphill. Right at the intersection there is a stairway at 130 Opera. The stairs only go to a single house that has a sign saying, "Hippies Use the Back Door." The tour will continue along Temby.

Stairways along Temby Avenue and Hunt Avenue

Almost immediately upon entering Temby Avenue, you'll run into your first stairway on the right going uphill at 1B Temby.

38. 1B Temby Avenue; 75 steps; Connects to a sidewalk leading to the 137 Opera stairway (# 37)

This stairway passes houses and abandoned building lots before reaching the sidewalk (at the top of the stairs) that leads to the 137 Opera stairway (# 37). The USA / WPA impression stamped in the concrete is readily visible.

39. 7A Temby Avenue; 95 steps; Connects to a path that leads to Keller Road

This stairway is very close to and very similar to the 1B Temby stairway (# 38). At the end of the stairway you can find a short path just beyond the small yard at the top of the steps. The path leads to the end of Keller Road which is just above you. The end of Keller Road is like a dirt parking lot below the High Road Overlook.

Once you reach Keller you have many options. You can walk across the parking area and find the 21 Temby stairway (# 41). Or you can walk up the very steep Keller Road to High Road. There you have the choice of going to the trailhead to hike or to continue down High Road to several more stairways.

For purposes of this guidebook the tour will return to Temby.

When you reach 12 Temby, the road will curve to the right. As you make the turn there will be a stairway going downhill on your left.

40. 12 Temby Avenue; 65 steps; Connects to 5 Clawson Avenue

   This stairway passes houses on its way down to Clawson. The building at the bottom of the stairs (to the left as you go down) was once the convent for St. Joseph Parish (the building is still identified as St. Joseph). It is now extended-stay lodging. There is a former church on your right that has been renovated into a residence. You can reach the intersection of Clawson and Opera by turning left at the bottom of the stairs.

41. 21 Temby Avenue; 117 steps; Connects to Keller Road (High Road)

   This stairway is on the right-hand side of Temby and goes uphill to Keller Road (High Road). As you go up, you'll pass houses and another stairway leading off to a house away from the stairs. The stairs end at Keller Road, which almost feels more like a steep driveway than a road. If you walk across the parking area at the end of Keller, you can find the trail that leads down to the 7A Temby stairway (# 39). If you turn left and walk up Keller, you'll reach the High Road Overlook at the end of High Road. There are several more stairways along High Road.

   There are incredible views of Bisbee from the High Road Overlook. The overlook is also the trailhead for hiking trails going west to Laundry Hill and also going north above Brewery Gulch to Zacatecas Canyon. (For more information, see *Hikes from the High Road Overlook* on page 89.)

42. 31 Temby Avenue; 75 steps; Connects to 25 Clawson Avenue

   This stairway is on the left-hand side of the road and is Stairway # 4 of the Bisbee 1000. It curves down to Clawson Avenue. There are houses and examples of funky folk art all along the way. The stairway ends across the

The Bisbee Stairs 53

street from the old 1913 Bisbee High School building. It is now a county office building.

As mentioned at the beginning of this guide, all four floors of the old high school have a ground level entrance. If you go to the front door of the school, you can find a plaque (a gift from the Class of 1948 on their 50th reunion) that mentions that the school's distinctive feature was once the subject of a "Ripley's Believe It or Not" cartoon.

43. 37 Temby Avenue; 151 steps; Connects to High Road

This stairway is across the street and a little bit to the west of the 31 Temby stairway (# 42). It is Stairway # 5 of the Bisbee 1000. It is a straight shot up to the top. Depending on how you count the terrace levels, there are four or five levels of houses.

There are also paths going off on either side of the stairway. To your left there is a very unusual shell of an old concrete building. When you near the top, keep your eyes open for a giant flower on your right. Once you reach the top you will not be too far from the 21 Temby stairway (# 41).

Again there are incredible views of Bisbee from the top of the stairway and on the hiking trails at the end of High Road.

Returning to Temby, the tour will continue west. Temby soon comes to an end as it reaches a junction with Hunt Avenue. For the tour, you'll make a right-hand turn and go uphill on Hunt. The road is very short, and the houses still have a Temby Avenue address. Just past the second house on the right, there is a stairway going uphill.

44. 45 Temby Avenue; 54 steps; Stub ending

These stairs are rather obscure. The USA/WPA impression in the concrete, however, is very evident. The stairs twist and turn past houses until they reach private property at the 54th step. At one time these stairs went all the way to High Road. If the owner of the house at the top of the stairs is around, he might take you through his yard and let you climb a twisting flight of stairs on his property up to High Road. The yard is an absolute gem. Since this is Bisbee, this should not come as a surprise.

45. End of Hunt Avenue Stairway; 72 steps; Stub ending

This stairway is a little past the 45 Temby stairway (# 44) and at the very end of Hunt. There is a sign at the bottom of the stairway saying that it is a private stairway. The sign is not clear if the stairs are privately owned, or if the stairs only lead to private homes. The stairs wind up a drainage and are quite pleasant until you reach a no trespassing sign. Because of the uncertainty of the stairway's ownership, this stairway can be skipped. There are many other stairways for you to climb.

From here you'll turn around and follow Hunt down the hill. The lower portion of the road has a nine-step sidewalk stairway. Hunt ends at its intersection with Shearer Avenue.

Stairways along Shearer Avenue

If you turn left from Hunt Avenue and follow Shearer downhill you'll soon be back at the old Bisbee High School, where Shearer crosses Clawson, and will not pass any stairways. Even though there is a dead end sign to your right, you can ignore it and head uphill. One of the great things about being on foot is that warning signs such as "Dead End" do not apply to you. If anything, a dead end sign should be your cue to keep going. This road happens to be very steep, but it does have a stairway at its end.

46. 85 Shearer Avenue; 80 steps; Connects to 44 High Road

This stairway follows a shady drainage up to High Road. You will pass houses on both sides of the stairway on your way up. The top portion of the stairway has been rebuilt and the house closest to the top is available to rent for a getaway or vacation stay. As you get towards the top look for the beetle painted on the retaining wall below High Road and for the Samoan quarter pressed into the concrete.

If you make a right-hand turn at High Road you can double back to the 21 and 37 Temby stairways (#'s 41 & 43). For this tour you'll turn left and follow High Road downhill.

Stairways along High Road

As you head downhill you'll soon see a short sidewalk on your left. It leads to a stairway that almost looks private because of the fencing and framing at the entrance of the stairway. It's a little used shortcut to the junction of High Road and Clawson Avenue down below.

47. 68 High Road; 77 steps; Connects with High Road just before its junction with Clawson

This stairway is obscure both at the top and at the bottom and has limited use. The stairway connects the two legs of a very sharp hairpin turn made by High Road.

Bottom of 68 High Road stairway (#47).

Once you pass through the gate at the top of the stairs, the stairway goes down to a house and then turns left. The last portion of the stairway is shaded and has a gentle grade. You'll also find a soil remediation project, great vegetation, and another house along this part of the stairway. The bottom of the stairway is next to the "Dead End" sign for High Road.

Continuing on High Road from the top of the stairway, you'll come upon another stairway on your right at 129 High Road.

48. 129 High Road; 50 steps; Stub ending

Some maps identify this stairway as Tank Hill Road. The stairway passes a house and leads up to a water tower. There is a trail at the top of the stairs that continues on to some abandoned building lots, an old mine opening, and excellent views of Bisbee.

Back on High Road you'll soon reach the same switchback that was mentioned in the description of 68 High Road stairway (# 47). You will see a house and a path in front of you where the switchback turns. The path is a "paper street" and a public right of way that leads to a stairway going down.

Ironman Ice Stairs (# 49) descending into the Courthouse Plaza District

49. Ironman Ice Stairs; 155 Steps; Connects to between 139 Clawson and 201 Tombstone Canyon (where Clawson Avenue joins Tombstone Canyon Road)

   The bottom of the stairway is immediately east of the Bisbee 1000 headquarters at 201 Tombstone Canyon. The stairway is used for the Ironman Ice Competition. For more information on the Ironman Ice Competition, please see *Bisbee 1000* on page 17.

   The stairway itself passes building lots, houses, and trails going off to the side. There's even an entrance to the second floor of the Bisbee 1000 building from the stairway.

If you make a right-hand turn at the bottom of the stairs and go up Clawson Avenue you'll soon find another stairway.

50. 127 Clawson Avenue; 51 steps; Stub ending

   This stairway makes a couple of turns as it leads up to two tiers of houses. This stairway is another example of how the organic nature of Bisbee's development has made it likely to find houses in the most unlikely of locations.

Courthouse Plaza District

So far this tour has covered the prominent stairways and trails in the Brewery Gulch area and the area above the central commercial district of old Bisbee. When you walked down the 155-step Ironman Ice Stairs you entered the Courthouse Plaza District. The joining of Tombstone Canyon Road and Clawson Avenue has made the road a bit wider and has given the area a plaza-like feeling.

There are several places to eat on both sides of the plaza and the 1931 art deco Cochise County courthouse is on the other side of the road. The Iron Man statue is also across the street and is in front of the courthouse. The copper color statue was erected in 1935 as a memorial to Bisbee's miners. It's worth walking over to the statue to read the dedication plaque and learn about "Those Virile Men" who worked in the mines. The Bisbee 1000 begins next to the statue and finishes by the side of the courthouse.

Iron Man statue and art deco courthouse in the Courthouse Plaza District. The Bisbee 1000 begins at the statue.

The Courthouse Plaza District is also where all three of the Bisbee stairway zones converge. From here you can head west along Tombstone Canyon Road to check out the stairways on the west and northwest side of Bisbee. Or you can start at the Iron Man statue and head to the east to cover the stairways of the Central Commercial District.

For purposes of this tour, the guidebook will cover the Central Commercial District first. You'll start by walking to the left of the statue and going uphill towards the County Administrative Building (it looks like and was at one time a school) on Ledge Avenue.

Stairways of Bisbee's Central Commercial District

The sidewalk on the west side of the County Building has a sign identifying it as Quality Hill Walk.

51. Quality Hill Walk; 88 steps; Connects to Quality Hill Road (west of Key Avenue)

    This stairway begins as a sidewalk through a small pleasant park on the west side of the County Building and is Stairway # 9 of the Bisbee 1000. At the end of the park the sidewalk becomes a stairway and passes several houses on its way up to Quality Hill Road. There is also another sign at the top identifying the stairway as Quality Hill Walk.

52. County Admin Building (east); 58 steps; Connects to Quality Hill Road (east of Key Avenue)

    This stairway begins as a sidewalk along the east side of the County Building and becomes a stairway leading to a parking area. The stairs continue up the hill and pass some houses before reaching a path that leads to Quality Hill Road.

The tour continues on Ledge Avenue and heads uphill toward the east. You'll stay on Ledge as it passes Cross Avenue and enters what seems like a parking area. As Ledge curves to the right to head south keep an eye out for 186 Ledge. You'll find a gravel walkway that leads to a stairway; there's even a small sign saying "Stairs."

53. 186 Ledge Avenue; 93 steps; Connects to 126 Tombstone Canyon Road across from Castle Rock

    To reach this stairway you'll follow the path that passes between two garages and then goes through a yard very close to someone's front door. Once you reach the stairs you'll have a steep descent into what seems like a canyon.

You'll be facing Castle Rock on the way down. Castle Rock is a large limestone formation that dominates this part of Bisbee. You'll also be descending into the western edge of the central business area. You can find several inns and places to eat by making a right-hand turn at the bottom of the stairs.

You'll also see the Bisbee 1000 logo painted on the side of the stairway at the bottom. There are small plaques honoring various friends of Bisbee's public stairways on the lower steps.

If you return to Ledge and continue walking south, Ledge will soon make a right-hand turn to end at Cross Avenue. At this point, Ledge is like an alley. If you turn left where Ledge turns right, you'll find a path at 114 Ledge that leads to a sidewalk that will soon become a stairway. You may also notice a house directly in front of you with the address of 78B.

54. 114 Ledge Avenue; 127 steps; Connects to 102 Tombstone Canyon Road (near Castle Rock and where Tombstone Canyon Road becomes Main Street)

This is Stairway # 8 of the Bisbee 1000. The stairway begins as a sidewalk with a few steps and then curves around at a reasonable grade to become a full-fledge stairway. The stairway passes houses as it curves all the way down to Tombstone Canyon Road.

You'll have great views of Castle Rock all along this stairway.

You'll have excellent views of Castle Rock and the road below the entire way. If you only have time to walk only one stairway in Bisbee's central business area, this is the one to walk!

Just before the sidewalk becomes a stairway, you'll see another stairway (#55) joining the sidewalk from the right.

The Bisbee Stairs

55. 186 Quality Hill Road; 28 steps; Connects to 114 Ledge Stairway (# 54)

This stairway can be found near the end of an alley-like street at the end of Quality Hill Road. When you reach 186 Quality Hill Road, follow the alley as it curves to the north past several houses.

The stairway has a nice gentle grade as it curves down to join the 114 Ledge stairway (# 54). This is a very pleasant walk and can be combined with the 114 Ledge stairway (# 54) for a 150-step or so stair climb.

You'll have a nice pleasant walk along this stairway

At the bottom of the stairway you can make a short detour to the left. After passing the bottom of the 186 Ledge stairway (# 53) you can continue around the curve and see a set of stairs at 130 Tombstone Canyon Road. Today the stairs go up to a locked gate. But if you look closely, you can see that at one time other stairways probably connected this stairway all the way up to Ledge Avenue. This is another example of how the stairways were built as a network to reach every corner of Bisbee.

Returning back to the bottom of the 114 Ledge steps (#54), keep heading east on Main Street.

56. 81 Main Street; 181 steps; Connects to 20 Maxfield Avenue at the top of Castle Rock

This stairway begins in a storefront on the north side of the street and is Stairway # 3 of the Bisbee 1000. The bottom of the stairway has been tattooed (decorated) with the Bisbee 1000 theme. This happens to be the tallest and one of the most interesting stairways in Bisbee.

The stairway begins almost as a tunnel through the store building. But you'll soon pop through the roof and be outside. Once outside you'll keep going up and be entering the world of funkiness. Every house and garden you pass will be worth a stop. One of the houses even uses an automobile door as its front gate.

The stairway makes several turns and passes three levels of houses before it reaches Maxfield. You'll even see side paths leading off to other houses. Some of those paths may be worth exploring.

When you reach Maxfield, you can turn left and walk to the top edge of Castle Rock. There you can look down on Tombstone Canyon Road and the Iron Man statue. (You'll pass some garages before you reach the edge.)

If you turn right, Maxfield will soon make a left-hand turn and become a brick alley that leads down toward the top level of the old four-story high school. Before reaching the school there will be a stairway to your left.

57. 13 Maxfield Avenue; 50 steps; Stub ending

This short stairway leads to several houses and is a good example of how the stairways have allowed people to build houses on a hillside with very few roads.

From this point you can continue toward the school or you can turn right into the parking area/alley above the backside of the school. Before turning into the alley, it is worthwhile to walk a few more steps toward the school to look down on an incredible koi pond on the right-hand side of the road.

The Bisbee Stairs   63

This pond is one of the many surprises you'll find in Bisbee when you get out and start walking. The pond was built out of large river cobbles by a life-long Bisbee resident. It has continuously circulating water and can be reached by a private stairway also built out of stone.

After checking out the koi, you can backtrack a bit and turn into the parking area above the backside of the school. If you follow the

This is only a small portion of the Fred Albert wall.

This is the garage next to the Fred Albert wall.

alley downhill and to the right, you'll find an amazing folk art wall created by the artist Fred Albert.

Albert was a successful artist who moved to Bisbee when he retired. The wall was one of his many retirement projects. Although Albert died in 2010, the legacy of his wall remains, and the wall is one more reason to slow down and take your time.

Albert lived in the house west of the wall, and if you walk towards the house, you'll find another stairway.

58. 59C Maxfield Avenue (this stairway is also called the Subway Stairs); 141 steps; Stub ending and Connects to 59 Subway Street

If you turn right and go up the stairs, you can climb 40 steps and pass several houses to a stub end. If you turn left, you can descend 101 steps and pass other houses as the stairway curves down to the central commercial area. 59 Subway is identified as the American Legion Building. Main Street is off to the right. You may be interested in the artwork on the building immediately to the right.

The tour continues by turning left on Subway Street. At the end of the building, Subway will veer to the right, and Tack Avenue will go to the left. There is a small sidewalk stairway at the end of the building that is not included in the 82 stairway count.

If you turn left and keep walking behind the building, Tack Avenue will turn right and head uphill. If you keep walking straight behind the commercial buildings the road becomes a path-like alley called Angius Avenue. Don't expect to find a street sign to tell you this.

You'll know you're at Angius Avenue by the two winged creatures guarding the steps leading to the historic Angius House. As you walk up the alley, and I certainly cannot imagine a car being able to navigate this very short roadway, you'll be greeted by other creatures and surprises along the way. At the end of this shaded canyon-like trek, you'll soon find a small shady grove with a stairway heading up to the next level. At this point you are right behind the lowest level of the old high school.

The Bisbee Stairs

Angius Avenue

59. Angius Stairs; 46 steps; Connects to a path and also to a sidewalk leading to the front of the old high school

   There are two choices at the end of the alley. One is to follow a short landscaped path to a residence. The other is to climb the 14-step flight of stairs to the backside of the old high school.

   When you reach the backside of the school, you can follow the brick sidewalk in front of you to a path that crosses private property. This path will take you back up to the Fred Albert folk art wall. If you stay on the brick sidewalk, you will reach a gate just below the koi pond.

   Or you can make a right-hand turn after climbing the 14 steps and climb 32 more steps to a sidewalk that leads to the front side of the old high school. The combination of the 14 steps and 32 steps creates a 46-step stairway.

The sidewalk along the old high school will take you to the intersection of Shearer Avenue and Clawson Avenue. Stairway # 4 of the Bisbee 1000 (# 42) is across the street. The Methodist Church is to the east on Clawson, and the Episcopal Church is down the hill off of Shearer. The tour will follow Clawson toward the Methodist Church.

You'll find the next stairway (#60) east of the Methodist Church.

60. 19 Clawson Avenue (next to Methodist Church); 44 steps; Stub ending

   This stairway begins immediately next to the church and leads to the church's front door. It then continues past the church to several houses and a stub end.

61. 9 Clawson Avenue; 26 steps; Connects to the end of Church Street

   This short stairway is across the street from the house on Clawson that used to be a church and is just before the bottom 12 Temby stairway (# 40). It leads down to Church Street. Church Street is a short connector street to Opera Drive.

The Bisbee Stairs

From the bottom of the steps you'll walk past the old Central School to Shearer Avenue and cut back towards the Episcopal Church. If you poke around between the Episcopal Church and the old high school you can find a sidewalk that goes to a large secluded house, a stairway that is no longer usable going down to another level, and a Japanese-style garden. I'm sure there is more for you to find in this maze-like area.

If you walk across the parking lot in front of the Episcopal Church you'll find a 25-step stairway that connects the parking lot to Tack Avenue. These stairs are in poor repair and are very twisted. They are not included in the 82 stairway count.

You are now very close to Main Street and can take several routes to get there. If you need one more stairway in the area, there is a small 15-step stairway between the Copper Queen Hotel and the Mining and Historical Museum. (This stairway, too, is not included in the 82 stairway count.) Once you're on Main, it's a short walk back to the Courthouse Plaza District.

Stairways West and Northwest of the Courthouse Plaza District along Tombstone Canyon Road

I have always found walking along Tombstone Canyon Road west of the Courthouse Plaza District to be very pleasant. Since the highway goes around old Bisbee rather than through town, most of the traffic on Tombstone Canyon is local. It is very quiet for a major street. And with Emory oaks along the way, there is plenty of shade to keep the walk comfortable.

You will run into your first stairway on Tombstone Canyon Road almost immediately. It is across the street from the Iron Man statue and on the west side of High Desert Market.

62. 203 Tombstone Canyon Road; 67 steps; Stub ending

> This stairway is on the west side of the group of buildings that includes High Desert Market and the Bisbee 1000 headquarters. The Ironman Ice stairs are on the east side of the buildings. This stairway leads to three terrace levels of houses and abandoned building lots.

As you continue west along Tombstone Canyon Road, you will soon reach an alley on the right-hand side of the road between 225 and 301 Tombstone Canyon. There is a stairway at the end of the alley.

63. 225 Tombstone Canyon Road; 92 steps; Stub ending

    This is a nice shaded stairway with USA / WPA stamped into the concrete. There are also some very interesting homes along the way. On the right-hand side of the stairway there is a private footbridge over a steep drainage leading to a home. On the left-hand side there is a great craftsman home from the early 1900s that may be a Sears kit home.

Returning to Tombstone Canyon Road, you'll pass an apartment building at 305 Tombstone, only two buildings west of the stairway (# 63). It was once a Mormon Church. In less than a block you'll reach the Jonquil Motel. The Jonquil is an old-style motel that has been renovated into more upscale lodgings. Across the street from the Jonquil is a stairway going up to O'Hara Avenue.

64. 317 Tombstone Canyon Road; 39 steps; Connects to 318 O'Hara

    This stairway goes up from Tombstone Canyon to a path that leads to O'Hara Avenue. According to a recent real estate listing, the house at 309 O'Hara (the second house on your left) is a Sears kit home. Many of the homes in Bisbee were built from kits.

When you return to Tombstone Canyon Road you'll soon see a Circle K convenience store on the north side of the road. As strange as it may seem, the Circle K is an important landmark for exploring this part of Bisbee. There is a stairway across the street from the Circle K next to the bus stop.

65. Bus Stop Stairs (across from the Circle K); 30 steps; Connects to O'Hara

    This short stairway connects to the end of O'Hara Avenue. If you want, you can walk back to the stairs at 318 O'Hara to return to Tombstone Canyon.

The tour will continue along Tombstone Canyon Road to explore the left-hand (south) side of the road and then return to the Circle K to explore the other side of the road. While walking along Tombstone Canyon Road, you've probably noticed the large concrete lined culvert that has been on the right-hand side of the road.

The culvert was built in the early part of the twentieth century to channel flood water in the Tombstone Canyon drainage around development. The culvert will switch to the left-hand side of the road and then back to the right-hand side as you get further up the road. You'll also see plenty of flat concrete bridges crossing the culvert. Many of the bridges were built during the Great Depression and have USA / WPA stamped in the concrete.

As you continue, you'll soon cross Mason Hill Road. Mason Hill is a short, steep, narrow street that is well suited for a mountain goat. There are plenty of stairs, but they all lead to single homes. There is a passageway towards the end of Mason Hill at 404C that leads up to the next tier of homes. Although Mason Hill does not have a stairway that we can explore, it does have some very interesting homes and great outdoor decoration.

In fact, every street in Bisbee, whether it has stairways or not, is interesting and worth exploring. When it comes to exploring and wandering, you can never make a wrong turn in Bisbee. Since this tour is about finding stairways, you'll continue on to the next street, Perley, and make a left-hand turn. There are stairs at the end of Perley.

66. Perley Street Stairs (416 Tombstone Canyon); 96 steps; Connects to 434 Roberts Avenue

Perley Street, like Mason Hill, is very steep and more like an alley than a street. Stairway # 7 of the Bisbee 1000 is at the end of the street. There is a painting depicting the race on the retaining wall at the corner of Tombstone Canyon and Perley. There is a picture of the wall on page 19.

On the right-hand side of the stairway there is a concrete culvert with five small, flat concrete bridges leading to the different levels of houses and building lots along the stairway. Both the stairway and Roberts Avenue up above are very shaded and pleasant to walk. If you turn right on Roberts, you can find another stairway (# 69) at the end of Roberts leading down to Brophy Avenue.

As you walk along Tombstone Canyon Road, the next street after Perley is Evans Avenue. Evans like Perley is a very short and steep street with a stairway at the end of it.

67. Evans Street Stairs (420 Tombstone Canyon); 62 steps; Stub ending

This stairway almost looks like a private stairway until you notice that it keeps twisting and turning to reach several levels of houses.

Brophy Avenue is the next street. Immediately to your left at 424 Tombstone Canyon is a sidewalk stairway going up on the east side of Brophy.

68. Brophy Sidewalk Stairway (424 Tombstone Canyon); 105 steps; Stub ending

This stairway begins as a sidewalk stairway at Tombstone Canyon Road. After you climb 38 steps, there is a brief gap in the stairway as Brophy curves off to the west. Within a few feet, the sidewalk stairway resumes as it curves around a parking area above and to the east of the Brophy turn. Please note that there is a sign in the parking area saying that it is private property. The sign applies to the parking area and not to the stairs.

The sidewalk stairway continues past a house and then becomes a regular stairway that leads up to more houses. The USA / WPA impression stamped into the concrete is readily visible.

Everything and anything can be used to decorate a house in Bisbee.

If you backtrack to where Brophy Avenue turns to west, you'll find another stairway down the street.

69. 505 Brophy Avenue; 90 steps; Connects to the end of Roberts Avenue

This stairway begins with a short flight of 11 steps to a sidewalk. The sidewalk leads to a steeper flight of 79 steps that finishes at the end of Roberts. You'll notice that some of the steps are not flat and quite twisted. Don't worry; they're still usable. Just watch your step.

There are houses and paths off to the side of the stairway. Like the Perley stairway, this stairway, too, is shady and like a little paradise. When you reach the top, you can turn left and walk back to the Perley stairway to take the stairs back down to Tombstone Canyon Road.

If you continue on Brophy Avenue to the west, the road will curve to the right and return to Tombstone Canyon Road. At the junction of Brophy and Tombstone Canyon, there is a stairway and sidewalk combination on the left-hand side of Brophy that ramps up to a terrace-level sidewalk with houses that face Tombstone Canyon Road. I suspect that at one time the sidewalk continued to a school that is no longer open and (at the time of this writing) is now for sale.

It's now time to walk back to the Circle K. Although it is not readily apparent, Art Avenue is in front of the Circle K and heads (north) through a narrow drainage. To find Art Avenue look for the dead end sign. Because it is so steep and narrow, Art Avenue is much easier to walk than drive.

You can find the bottom of the first Art Avenue stairway in the Circle K parking lot. This stairway is very easy to miss, but if you look for an opening between two garages, you'll see a short sidewalk leading to some stairs.

70. 15 Art Avenue; 164 steps; Connects to Laundry Hill Road

When I first saw this stairway, I thought that it only led to one house. It never occurred to me that the stairway would change direction more than six times on its way to the top of Laundry Hill. The addresses of the houses at the top of the stairs are 17F and 17G, which represent the sixth and seventh terrace level of houses along the stairway.

You'll find the bottom of the stairway between two garages facing the Circle K parking lot.

When you do get to the top, you'll discover that finding the stairway from the top is even harder than finding it at the bottom. Your only clue is a fire hydrant off to the left of a house at the end of Laundry Hill Road. Once you spot the fire hydrant, look for a gravel path. It leads around a house and under a deck to reach the top of the stairway.

As you walk on the stairway, keep an eye out for an old fashion wringer washing machine in one of the backyards. Can you think of a better way to decorate a house on Laundry Hill than to stick an old washing machine in the backyard? This is truly a very interesting and secret stairway.

When you reach the top of Laundry Hill you'll see the top of the 503 Mayer stairway (# 72) on the other side of the street. Further up on the right-hand side of this very short street, you'll see where the 29 Art Avenue stairway (# 71) reaches the top of Laundry Hill. It's just beyond and above the house with the address of 29E.

Old washing machine along the stairway on Laundry Hill.

If you keep walking, Laundry Hill Road will angle to the left to become Adams Avenue. Adams runs along the side of the hill well above Tombstone Canyon Road. If you continue along Adams a short distance to where it slightly dips for a drainage, you can find an unmarked trailhead. (For more information see *Hikes from the Adams Avenue Trailhead* on page 91.)

The tour will return to the Circle K and continue up Art Avenue. You'll pass stairways on either side of the road that only go up to a single-terrace level of houses. Very soon there will be a 36-step sidewalk stairway on the left-hand side of the road. Towards the middle of the sidewalk stairway there is another stairway going uphill to the left.

71. 29 Art Avenue; 144 steps; Connects to Laundry Hill Road

This is a very steep stairway that ends at a path above the house at 29E Art Avenue; that's five terrace levels above Art Avenue. The short path joins Laundry Hill Road very close to where it turns into Adams. Most of the houses along this stairway have been removed and considerable soil remediation has been done in this area.

If you do not want to go back down this stairway (#71), you can turn left and take the 503 Mayer Ave stairway (# 72) down or go down the 15 Art Avenue stairway (# 70). Another option is to walk along Adams to the trailhead or go further on Adams to the Gladys stairway (# 75) that will take you back down to Tombstone Canyon Road.

The tour continues from the Circle K and proceeds along Garden Avenue which is immediately to the left of the Circle K. It is almost like an alley for Tombstone Canyon Road. Just before Garden rejoins Tombstone Canyon, Mayer Avenue will go off to the right. Since there are stairways on Mayer, the tour will follow Mayer.

72. 503 Mayer Avenue; 136 steps; Connects to Laundry Hill Road

This is Stairway # 6 of the Bisbee 1000. The stairway is plenty steep, but it is not as steep as some of the others. At one time this stairway route was a road that must have been very steep and narrow. I can't imagine anything other than a mule being able to use it.

This stairway reaches six levels of housing with the highest level being 501F Mayer. All along the way you'll see stairs and paths branching off from either side to reach houses away from the stairs. When you get closer to the top you'll run into a metal sculpture of a dragon and a sign announcing Dragonview Mountain Retreat.

This used to be a road.

The Retreat is a complex of houses connected by a fabulous stone stairway. Unfortunate-

Part of the Dragonview complex

ly that stairway is private. From the public stairway you can get a glimpse of the great stone work and several great places to sit. And I have to say it again and cannot say it enough, walking in Bisbee is like passing from one amazing personal Shangri-La to another.

The stairway reaches Laundry Hill Road almost across the street from the 15 Art Avenue stairway (# 70). The 29 Art Avenue stairway (# 71) is up the street and to the right. From here you can turn around, go down any of the Art Avenue stairs, or walk along Laundry Hill Road to the Adams trailhead for a hike, or go further along Adams to take the Gladys stairway (# 75) down to Tombstone Canyon.

73. 511 Mayer Avenue; 81 steps; Stub ending

    This stairway starts with a short flight of stairs to the first terrace level of houses. After a short walk the well shaded stairs ascend steeply to more houses and building lots.

Mayer Avenue rejoins Tombstone Canyon Road across the street from the same old school house that was mentioned when you were back at the intersection of Brophy and Tombstone Canyon. As Bisbee's population changed, the town's schools have been consolidated to locations on the other side of the pit. Two of the three former schools that you have already passed are now government office buildings. The third is now an art center. There is still another former school in front of you that is now an inn.

You'll soon reach another stairway on the right-hand side of Tombstone Canyon Road.

74. 534 Tombstone Canyon Road; 60 steps; Stub ending

    This stairway is reached by crossing a flat concrete WPA bridge over the culvert. The stairway has nice shade and leads to three levels of houses. There are paths going to houses away from the stairs. At the top of the stairs there is a short sidewalk with a colorful wall showing the addresses of the nearby houses.

As you continue along Tombstone Canyon Road, you'll soon reach Warren Hill Street on the left-hand side of the road. It is a steep road that borders the western edge of the old schoolhouse that was just mentioned. There is a 46-step sidewalk stairway on the other side of the street after you pass the school building. Although the steps have had recent repairs, they are almost unusable because of overhanging shrubs.

Further up the road at 603 Tombstone Canyon Road you'll reach Gladys Avenue on the right-hand side of the road. It is a very small street with a stairway at the end.

75. Gladys Avenue Stairway (603 Tombstone Canyon); 143 steps; Connects to Adams Avenue

To reach these stairs, you'll cross the culvert on a concrete WPA bridge and pass two very nice homes on either side of the stairway bottom. The stairway goes up a steep drainage that is nicely shaded. There are several nice homes and empty terraces that have been turned into great gardens. You'll also see evidence of recent remediation projects. If you turn right on Adams when you reach the top, you can walk to the hiking trailhead or to the three stairways (#'s 70, 71, & 72) leading down from Laundry Hill.

After you return to Tombstone Canyon Road, you'll soon pass an old firehouse that was built in 1914. It is still used today. The road beyond the firehouse is Moon Canyon. Moon Canyon happens to be on the route of the Bisbee 1000. If you make a right-hand turn, you'll find a stairway at 5 Moon Canyon.

76. 5 Moon Canyon; 49 steps; Stub ending

This stairway leads to three terrace levels of houses and ends at a private property sign. The USA / WPA stamp in the concrete is readily visible. There is a small concrete lined drainage ditch on the side of the stairs.

The road (Moon Canyon) continues uphill and eventually reaches Adams Avenue. For exploring stairways you'll return to Tombstone Canyon Road. There is a stairway immediately across the street from the firehouse at 643 Tombstone Canyon.

77. 643 Tombstone Canyon Road; 64 steps; Stub ending

This stairway leads to houses, building lots, and a sidewalk that is now overgrown and unusable. At one time that sidewalk connected to a flight of stairs that went up to the end of Cantner Road. (Cantner Road was on your left just before you reached the firehouse.) If you walk up to the end of Cantner, you can still see the steps that once connected with the 634 Tombstone Canyon stairway. They are now private and go down to the house below.

As you walk up Tombstone Canyon Road, you'll reach Star Avenue on the right-hand side of the road. There are a couple of very subtle mine openings but no stairways along Star Avenue. Star Avenue does, however, intersect with the east end of Warren Avenue which runs parallel to and above Tombstone Canyon. For this tour you'll continue on Tombstone Canyon Road.

78. 729 Tombstone Canyon Road; 56 steps; Connects to 729 Warren

This stairway has new steps on the bottom and is a connector between the two roads.

Spring Canyon Road is across the street from the 729 Tombstone Canyon stairway and heads uphill. Like all of the streets on that side of the road, it is very steep. Although Spring Canyon does not have any stairways, it does have an interesting pedestrian tunnel going under the highway and a spectacular iron sculpture on the other

Sculpture on Spring Canyon Road.

side of the highway. So if you feel like a mountain goat, it's worth the walk.

79. 735 Tombstone Canyon Road; 76 steps; Connects to a path leading to Star Avenue

   This stairway is just beyond the junction of Warren and Tombstone Canyon. The stairway passes three levels of houses and building lots. There is a path going off to the left from the stairway that leads to houses that are not on the stairs.

   At the top of the stairway, there is a subtle path going off to the right and up. It cuts across an empty lot and leads to a branch of Star Avenue.

Returning to Tombstone Canyon Road, you'll soon see Gentry Avenue on the left-hand side of the road. If you walk up Gentry you'll see a short 14-step sidewalk stairway that ends at 800B Gentry. If you turn left and follow the alley-like ending of Gentry you'll find another stairway.

80. 734 Gentry Avenue; 41 steps; Connects to Pace Avenue

   This stairway ends at what almost seems like a paved driveway. If you continue going uphill, the driveway will join what seems like a narrow dirt country road. The road is actually Pace Avenue. You can follow Pace all the way down to Tombstone Canyon and will have commanding views of the area along the way.

   When you walk along Pace Avenue you will pass the last of the five former schools on this tour through old Bisbee. The former school is now an inn.

   The next stairway of the tour is on Sims Road which is very close to the intersection of Pace and Tombstone Canyon. Sims joins Pace opposite from the public park and the playground in front of the old school. You'll want to turn left on to Sims.

81. 826 Sims Road; 39 steps; Connects to the end of Sims Road

   Sims essentially doubles back on itself and these stairs connect the lower portion of Sims to the upper portion of Sims. There is a sign at the bottom of the stairway warning you to be careful when walking on the steps.

   Once you climb these steps, you'll return to Tombstone Canyon Road and proceed to 831 Tombstone Canyon. There you'll find a pump house on the right-hand side of the road. It pumps water to a reservoir on top of the hill above us. The building has a plaque noting that the WPA rebuilt the pump house in 1936. Behind the pump house and across the culvert on a flat concrete bridge is one of the nicest stairways in Bisbee.

82. Pump House Stairway (831 Tombstone); 111 steps; Connects to Locklin Avenue

   This stairway starts behind the pump house and winds its way up the hill through a shady grove of Emory oaks. At the top, you'll find outstanding views of Bisbee and a fenced in concrete reservoir. The reservoir provides water for the fire hydrants in this part of Bisbee. If you keep walking along the sidewalk beside the reservoir, you'll find a long abandoned concrete swim-

ming pool that was built during the Great Depression by the WPA.

If you continue past the swimming pool, you'll reach Locklin Avenue. Locklin goes back down to Tombstone Canyon. It is one half mile by road to the bottom of the stairway.

You are now in the far northwest end of Bisbee and have reached the last stairway. With this, the stairway tour of old Bisbee is finished.

Stairway Summary

This stairway tour of old Bisbee described 82 different stairways. Several other stairways and sidewalk stairways were mentioned in the narrative but are not included in the stairway count. If you happen to climb all 82 of the described stairways, you will have climbed 6478 steps for an average of 78 steps per stairway. That would be like climbing a 450 plus story building. No matter how you count it that is a lot of steps.

The tallest stairway in this guide is the 81 Main Street stairway with 181 steps. The shortest stairway is the Central School Alley stairway with 16 steps. 22 of the 82 stairways have over 100 steps. Many of the shorter stairways can be combined with other stairways to make for a climb of over 100 steps. If you are looking for a workout, you can find it in old Bisbee.

More important than any step count or how fast you go is what you see and experience while you wander around Bisbee. The value of the stairways is that they were built for walking and they give you a great reason to get out there and start exploring. Once you're out, it is up to you to allow yourself to get the most out of your adventure.

And even better, you can do all of this in what may be the most interesting small town in the country. There is no place like Bisbee. And as far as I am concerned, it is what Bisbee is today, and not what it was, that makes Bisbee a great place to visit again and again.

Trailhead at the end of OK Street

Section 3

Hikes from the Bisbee Trailheads

Hikes from the End of OK Street

The OK Street trailhead is at the northern end of OK Street. It is not marked and is very obscure. There is no parking at the end of OK Street. Fortunately, this is not a problem as you can park in the center of town and walk a half mile to the end of OK Street or you can park on Brewery Avenue near Mimosa Market and climb the 122 steps of the 215 Brewery Avenue (north) stairway (# 16) up to the trailhead. As an extra bonus, Mimosa Market is a good place to stop for snacks to take along on your hike.

> The GPS coordinates for the trailhead are: N 31°26'51.4"; W 109°54'45.5"

Once you reach the end of OK Street, you can find the trailhead by walking up the steep concrete driveway on the right-hand side of the street towards 238 OK Street. Before reaching the gate, step up on to the loose rock surface to the right of the drive. If you keep heading in the same direction as the driveway, you should see traces of the trail. There are a couple of small trails that branch off into dead ends or into fences, but if you poke around, you should find the right trail. It will soon become a very distinct trail.

Once you're on the on the trail, you'll have a very nice and peaceful walk high above where Brewery Gulch becomes Zacatecas Canyon.

You'll also be passing through some great high-desert landscape of Emory oaks, red bark manzanitas, yuccas, and ocotillos. If you happen to walk on a day after a rain, you can see the ocotillos starting to green up. Even better you might see the ocotillos with orange red flowers and leaves on their stem.

Ocotillo in bloom.

I have read that much of this wonderful trail is on private land. The area is currently open to hiking, but if it is private, it can be closed to hiking at any time. Please don't do anything to abuse the privilege or anything else to give any owners a reason to deny access. If you do come across a no trespassing sign, please respect it and do not trespass. We are lucky to have what is available to us.

After walking less than a quarter of a mile, you'll reach a rock cairn and a small white wooden cross.

GPS Coordinates for the cairn are: N 31°27'00.0"; W 109°54'42.1"

If you turn right and head uphill, you'll soon reach the cross and shrines at the top of Youngblood Hill. This is the cross that you can clearly see from much of Bisbee. The cross is approximately 370 feet above the trailhead and can be reached after a half mile of hiking. There is no one trail leading from the cairn to the top. It is more like a braid of small trails crisscrossing each other through the loose schist flakes. But if you keep heading up, you'll get there. Watch your footing on the loose rock.

Just before you reach the top you'll see beads and Tibetan prayer flags draped in the shrubs. You'll find several Buddhist shrines, including a picture of the Dali Lama, below the prayer flags. As you make the final ascent to the top, you'll find a whole complex of Hispanic and Catholic oriented shrines at the summit.

Bisbee from the shrine.

GPS Coordinates for the summit are: N 31°26'55.1";
W 109°54'38.1"

With its many nooks, niches, pictures, statues, and rosaries, the shrine surrounds the hilltop. As you poke around you'll come upon a plaque saying: "This shrine was built & maintained by Adolfo C. & Mary Vasquez – May, 1980."

As best as I can determine, Adolfo and Mary started building the shrine after Adolfo's eyesight began to fail. I also understand that his eyesight did improve and that he has since passed away. Whether this is true or not, the shrine is a remarkable achievement and a wonderful addition to what makes Bisbee special. It is also a tremendous hiking destination.

As you explore the summit area you'll find other shrines, benches for sitting, amazing views of Bisbee and the surrounding mountains, and even a built-in barbecue grill. It's all set for a picnic. But the shrine is not just a place to socialize or explore; it also a place for contemplation. When I first climbed to the shrine, I found a piece a paper lying on a bench with a very sobering poem that had a very startling line: "I saw a needle take another man."

If you wish, you can find more trails on top of the hill to continue your hike. If you do continue hiking make sure that you don't trespass or drift into an area closed to hiking. The land to the east of the shrine is owned by the mining company, Freeport-McMorRan.

If you return to the cairn and small cross at the bottom of the hill, you can go back to Bisbee or continue hiking north away from the trailhead. If you hike north, you'll have a wonderful and peaceful walk that comes to an end in one mile when you reach a fence with a no trespassing sign.

GPS Coordinates for the fence are: N 31°27'23.8"; W 109°54'54.7"

Along the way you'll pass a few mine openings and rock walls and dams built by the CCC during the Great Depression for flood and erosion control. The trail going north is well maintained with the yucca leaves trimmed away from the trail. Nothing says ouch like jamming your leg into the sharp point of a yucca leaf. There are also several small whimsical cairns along the way.

You'll find both hiking options from the end of OK Street to be great.

CCC check dams along the trail

Hikes from the High Road Overlook

The High Road Overlook is at the eastern end of High Road. Like the other trailheads of Bisbee, the High Road Overlook trailhead is not marked and very obscure. The overlook does have limited parking. You can also reach the area by climbing the 7A Temby, 21 Temby, or 37 Temby stairways (#'s 38, 41, & 43).

When you get to the High Road Overlook, there is a rock wall with an opening in it on the north side of the overlook. The wall provides an enclosure for another parking area. Once you orient yourself to the enclosure, you have two options for finding the trails.

The trail starts beyond this wall

The first is to walk through the enclosure to the northeast corner of the parking area. There you'll find a trail working its way through some old foundations to higher ground. The second is to climb the stairs in front of the enclosure wall to where they end above the nearby house. There is a trail at the end of stairs that also works its way through the old foundations. Both trail options come together in the middle of the old foundations.

The GPS coordinates for the trailhead area are:
N 31°26'40.2"; W 109°54'58.2"

The first part of the trail is like snaking yourself through a maze of old building foundations. Eventually the trail will become distinct and you'll reach a junction. From the junction you can head north and hike for around two thirds of a mile to Zacatecas Canyon. Or you can head west and hike a little less than three quarters of a mile to the Laundry Hill trailhead on Adams Avenue. Both trails have great views and are worth walking.

The GPS coordinates for the junction are: N 31°26'42.4"; W 109°54'59.1"

If you head north towards Zacatecas Canyon, you'll be high above the houses on the west side of Brewery Gulch. The views are outstanding, and the trail is very distinct as it passes through high-desert shrubs and grasses. You'll see remains of structures and will soon reach an old water tank within a quarter mile. Just beyond the tank is a junction with another trail. It leads down to the trailhead near 200 Upper Opera (see page 50).

The GPS coordinates for the junction with the Upper Opera trail are: N 31°26'48.7"; W 109°54'55.0"

A large rock at the junction has a very faint "Laundry Hill" marking painted on it along with an arrow pointing back in the direction you came from. Laundry Hill is about a mile away from this point. At one time this may have been the preferred route to connect these two parts of town.

Continuing north towards Zacatecas Canyon, you'll see several faint trails heading off in different directions. If you stay on the main trail, you'll soon pass an old mine opening that looks like someone may be living there or at least spending considerable time there. Not too long after that you'll reach the end of the trail in Zacatecas Canyon. From there you can follow Zacatecas Canyon road to Brewery Avenue or hike back on the trail.

The GPS coordinates for the junction with Zacatecas Canyon are: N 31°26'58.1"; W 109°54'51.5"

If you return to the first junction (the one closest to the High Road Overlook trailhead), you can check out the trail heading west to the Laundry Hill trailhead on Adams Avenue. The first part the trail heads uphill. It then levels out well above the buildings and houses along Tombstone Canyon Road. The trail is a little less than three fourths of a mile and has outstanding views the entire way.

Again you'll be passing through wonderful high-desert shrubs and grasses. If you look closely, you might spot alligator juniper. As you work your way around the side canyons you'll also be able to see many of the check dams built by the CCC for flood and erosion control during the Great Depression. At Art Avenue Canyon, the trail passes over one of the CCC dams. This is your clue that you are getting close to the trailhead on Adams Avenue.

The GPS coordinates for the Adams Avenue trailhead are: N 31°26'48.4"; W 109°55'28.3"

From the Adams Avenue trailhead you can continue hiking (see *Hikes from the Adams Avenue Trailhead* below), or you can walk on Adams Avenue. If you turn left you can take one of the three stairways (#'s 70, 71, & 72) on Laundry Hill back down to Tombstone Canyon Road. If you turn right you can take the Gladys Avenue stairway (# 75) back down to Tombstone Canyon Road.

Hikes from the Adams Avenue Trailhead

The Adams Avenue trailhead is just off of Adams Avenue near Laundry Hill. Like the other trailheads, the Adams Avenue trailhead is not marked. This trailhead, however, is more apparent than the OK Street and the High Road Overlook trailheads. To find this trailhead, walk down Adams Avenue from Laundry Hill to where it makes its first slight dip for a drainage. The trailhead is right there.

The GPS coordinates for the Adams Avenue trailhead are: N 31°26'48.4"; W 109°55'28.3"

There are two choices from this trailhead. One is to head east towards High Road. The other is to walk a few feet up to what looks like a very short road and then take a trail heading west. A description of the trail heading east can be found in *Hikes from the High Road Overlook Trailhead* on page 89. The trail heading west is less than a third of a mile long and rejoins Adams Avenue just above where it joins Moon Canyon. The end of the trail has a bit of a drop to reach Adams, so be careful.

**The GPS coordinates for the end of trail are:
N 31°26'57.0"; W109°55'37.7"**

From here you can return on the trail, or walk along Adams Avenue. If you turn left you can take the Gladys Avenue stairway (# 75) down to Tombstone Canyon Road. If you turn right, you can follow Adams downhill to where it joins Moon Canyon and follow Moon Canyon to Tombstone Canyon Road. The Adams to Moon Canyon route is part of the Bisbee 1000, so you might see some runners practicing for the race.

Afterword or How this Book Came to Be

I hope this guidebook has shown you how wonderful outdoor public stairways are for exploring and what a great place Bisbee is for wandering around. In my opinion, Bisbee is one of the most interesting, if not the most interesting, small town in America.

As for writing this guidebook, I first learned of outdoor public stairways when I read an article by Dan Koeppel in the September 2010 issue of **Backpacker Magazine** about a stairway walk he developed in Los Angeles. The idea of exploring a city on foot by climbing up and down public stairways intrigued me so much that I used a frequent flyer ticket to fly out to Los Angeles two weeks after reading the article to check them out. The two days I spent walking around Los Angeles and climbing stairways turned out to be one of the best trips of my life.

A month after the trip to Los Angeles, the October 2010 issue of **Runners World** ran an article by Stephanie Pearson about the Bisbee 1000. As mentioned in this guidebook, the Bisbee 1000 is an annual race that features running up nine of Bisbee's outdoor public stairways. Needless to say I made a detour to Bisbee to climb stairways the next time I traveled to Arizona.

Although I only had two hours to spend in Bisbee on that trip, I was hooked. The stairs were great and the town was amazing. No matter which way I turned there was something incredible to see and I knew I had to come back.

The trips to Los Angeles and Bisbee along with many other on foot

The Bisbee Stairs

adventures became the basis of my 2012 book, *The Gentle Art of Wandering*. Wandering, as described in the book, is letting what you see guide you on where you go. It is really about being mindful when walking. When you adopt the mindset of wandering you will always discover something and have an amazing adventure every time you go out.

Since climbing stairways in Los Angeles and Bisbee, I have climbed stairways and explored the hidden corners of many towns across the country. You can read about many of those walks in my wandering blog at www.gentleartofwandering.com. In fact I encourage you to visit the blog frequently as there is always something new to read.

To write this guidebook, my dog Petey and I made several trips to Bisbee and spent many, many days walking every street in old Bisbee, most of them several times, and climbing every stairway we found. We also spoke to city officials and residents and read whatever materials we could find to learn as much we could about Bisbee and its stairways.

I hope you have found the resulting guidebook to be informative and comprehensive. I also hope you enjoyed or will enjoy walking around Bisbee as much as I have and do.

As a mild disclaimer, the descriptions in this guide are accurate, to the best of my knowledge, as of May 2014. It is always possible that a stairway or path described in this guidebook may be altered or closed to the public by the time you explore Bisbee. If you do find a No Trespassing or Private Property sign on a described stairway or pathway, don't despair. There are plenty of others out there for you to explore. You won't be disappointed.

Informal Source List

Most of the information in this book is a result of actually walking every street of old Bisbee and climbing every stairway I encountered and by talking to people along the way. I did, however, consult many written resources both online and hardcopy. They include:

AZ Sphinx Moth. "The Dirt I Occupy: Mining Town Dirt." *The Daily Kos*, January 16, 2012.

"Bisbee Residential Historic District." *National Register of Historic Places: Registration Form*, 2010.

Carter, Bill. *Boom, Bust, Boom: A Story about Copper, the Metal that Runs the World*. New York: Scribner. 2012.

Pearson, Stephanie. "Step it Up: More than 1,000 Stairs Have Runners Scrambling in this Arizona 5-K." *Runners World*, October 2010.

Ring, Bob. *Warren, Arizona – The City Beautiful*. Paper presented to the Arizona History Convention (Pine Top, Arizona), April 28, 2001.

Sullivan, Michael. "Shrines Above Bisbee Created Out of Love, Faith." *The Sierra Vista Herald*, February 12, 2006.

"The WPA in Bisbee." *The Copper Chronicle*; KBRP Radio, October 23, 2012.

"The Stairways of Bisbee." *Newsletter*; Bisbee Mining and Historical Museum, Issue #57 Summer/Fall 2007.

Trillin, Calvin. "U.S. Journal: Bisbee, Arizona; Ground Floor." *The New Yorker*, March 3, 1975.

Stairways in Other Communities

Bisbee is not the only community in the country with outdoor public stairways. If a town has hills, there is a good chance that it has a stairway or several stairways. Within the state of Arizona, the old mining towns of Globe, Miami, and Jerome have stairways. None of those three come close to matching Bisbee's network. But mining towns are not the only places to look for stairways. Los Angeles, California happens to have over 300 and Pittsburgh, Pennsylvania, with over 700 stairways, has the most.

I personally have climbed outdoor public stairways in Arizona, California, District of Columbia, Georgia, Illinois, Iowa, Kansas, Minnesota, New York, North Carolina, Ohio, Oregon, Pennsylvania, Tennessee, Virginia, West Virginia, and Wisconsin. In fact, when I travel I make it a point to look for stairways. As mentioned earlier, you can read about many of these stairway walks in my wandering blog at www.gentleartofwandering.com.

If you are interested in learning more about stairways in other communities, you can begin by visiting www.PublicStairs.com. The website is the creation of Doug and Joan Beyerlein, and is a clearinghouse for information on stairways. The site also has a directory of stairways with maps.

I have found the following books to be helpful for many of my stair climbs.

Bakalinsky, Adah. *Stairway Walks in San Francisco: The Joy of Urban Exploring*. Birmingham: Wilderness Press. 2010.

Berkeley Path Wanderers Association. *A Map of Berkeley's Pathways*. 2009.

Fleming, Charles. *Secret Stairs: A Walking Guide to the Historic Staircases of Los Angeles*. Santa Monica: Santa Monica Press. 2010.

Foster, Laura O. *The Portland Stairs Books*. Portland: Timber Press. 2010.

Inman, Bob. *Finding Los Angeles by Foot: Stairstreet, Bridge, Pathway and Lane*. 2013.

Inman, Bob. *A Guide to the Public Stairways of Los Angeles*. Blurb Books. 2010.

Koeppel, Dan. "The Big Parade." *Backpacker Magazine*, September, 2010.

Koeppel, Dan. "I Climbed Los Angeles." *Backpacker Magazine*, June 2004.

Jaramillo, Jake and Cathy. *Seattle Stairway Walks*. Seattle: The Mountaineers Books. 2013.

Acknowledgements

Although the research and writing of this guidebook was done by me, I had considerable help along the way. First of all I want to thank my dog Petey for accompanying me on my trips to Bisbee and for climbing every stairway along the way. I am especially grateful to Andy Haratyk from the City of Bisbee for taking the time to tell me about Bisbee and its stairs and for letting me look at some of the old survey maps of Bisbee. I am also indebted to Cynthia Conroy for sharing the story of the Bisbee 1000 with me.

On actually turning Petey's and my research into something you can read, I want to thank my wife Claudia for helping me with the writing and shaping my thoughts into a manuscript. I want to thank my sister Carolyn Ryan for turning the manuscript and pictures into a book that you can actually pick up and read. And I want to thank Jodi McGrath of the Cochise County GIS Department for helping me turn my notes and chicken scratches into a legible map of Bisbee.

Thanks to all of the people of Bisbee who talked to me on my many walks and to the staff members of Bisbee Vogue who provided me pictures and additional information on the Bisbee 1000. I finally want to thank Bob Inman, the author of two guidebooks to Los Angeles' stairways, and Bob Julyan, author of many walking and other books, for their thoughts and encouragement on this guide.

Contact Information:

Contact the Author
David Ryan
612-889-9640
davidryan@msn.com
www.gentleartofwandering.com
www.newmountainbooks.com

Ordering Information:

Call: 612-889-9640
E-mail: davidryan@msn.com
Write:
New Mountain Books
2324 Rio Grande Boulevard NW
Albuquerque, NM 87104
www.newmountainbooks.com